Instruction Guidebook

INTRODUCING MANUSCRIPT MANUSCRIPT TRANSITION CURSIVE

An Instructor's Guidebook For Use With:

God Made My World
Words of Promise
Words of Jesus
Words to Live By

Words of Love
Words of Praise
Words of Wisdom

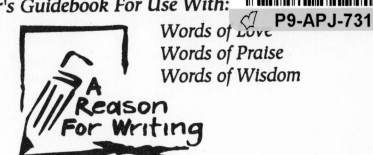

A
Reason
For Writing

A Concerned Communications Publication

Welcome to *A Reason For Writing!*

A Reason For Writing is the most complete Scripture-based handwriting curriculum available. Students will not only have the opportunity to improve their handwriting skills, but will find themselves learning meaningful Scripture passages and having an opportunity to share them with others as well.

This Teacher's Guide is organized so that each section can stand independently. For multigrade classrooms, having the complete Teacher's Guide for the series in one book is very practical.

Teachers of larger schools will also find it useful as they can use the other sections for remedial or acceleration help.

Don't miss the added bonus of black line masters for handwriting paper identical to that used in the Student Workbooks. These are found at the back of each section along with evaluation forms and a form letter to send with the Border Sheets.

May God bless you as you touch lives for Him!

Concerned Communications
Publishers of
A REASON FOR WRITING

Table of Contents

Authors:
Carol Ann Retzer
Eva Hoshino

Editors:
Patricia Horning Benton

Art Director:
Walt Woesner
Mark Ford

Illustrators:
Mary Bausman

General Guidelines for Teaching A Reason For Writing

God Made My World

Words of Promise

Words of Jesus

Words to Live By

Words of Love

Words of Praise

Words of Wisdom

A Reason For Writing

Scripture Verses That Make Handwriting Fun!

Kindergarten

1st Grade

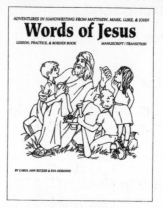
2nd Grade

3rd Grade

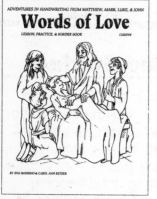
4th Grade

5th Grade

6th Grade

Teacher's Guide

The Series

A Reason for Writing is a classroom-tested program providing complete handwriting instruction for elementary grades, using Scripture verses. With one textbook on the kindergarten level, two textbooks on the manuscript level, two textbooks on the transition level, and three textbooks in cursive, Christian schools can now put together their own curriculum options using either a rotating cycle or a book for each grade.

Introduction to Manuscript
(Suggested for Kindergarten & Pre-first)
✎ God Made My World (Creation)

Manuscript
✎ Words Of Promise (Psalms & Proverbs)

Manuscript/Transition
✎ Words Of Jesus (The Gospels)

Transition
✎ Words To Live By (New Testament Epistles)

Cursive
✎ Words Of Love (The Gospels)
✎ Words of Praise (Psalms)
✎ Words of Wisdom (Proverbs)

Goals

There are three major goals of *A Reason For Writing*. First, of course, is to help each student develop good handwriting skills. Second is to provide character-building handwriting lessons for elementary students. Third is to encourage each student to share God's Word with others.

Bible Version

After comparing several different versions of the Bible, *The Living Bible* was selected for use in *A Reason For Writing.* The simple vocabulary used in this version makes it especially understandable for children.

Body Position

A good writing position provides comfort and balance. When writing at his or her desk, a student should be encouraged to:

- ✎ Sit comfortably back in the seat, facing the desk squarely.

- ✎ Place feet flat on the floor.

- ✎ Lean slightly forward, but without letting the body touch the edge of the desk.

- ✎ Rest both forearms on the desk.

- ✎ Hold the paper firmly in place with free hand.

Paper Placement

Both left and right-handed students should learn the same principle of paper placement. Instruct the student to place the paper at the same angle as the arm he uses for writing. *(See illustrations.)* Demonstrate for the class or the individual student how the page can easily be moved up as the writing nears the bottom of the page. Emphasize this paper positioning for both manuscript and cursive writing.

Pencil Position

The pencil should be held loosely, above the sharpened point. Instruct the student to grasp the pencil between the thumb and index finger, letting it rest lightly on the middle finger. Alert the student not to allow his fingers to slip down to the sharpened part of the pencil.

The Left-Handed Student

Special attention should be given to the left-handed child. From the start he should be taught to hold his pencil at least one-half inch above the sharpened part. This—combined with the correct slant of the paper—will enable him to see what he is writing, thus keeping him from adopting a hooked-hand position or an exaggerated tilt of the head.

Paper placement for a right-handed student.

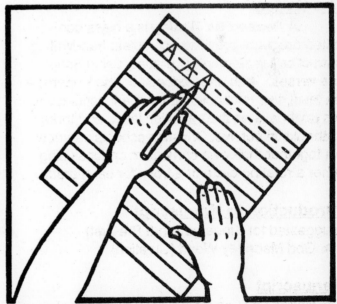

Paper placement for a left-handed student.

Philosophy

For all of us, children and adults alike, writing is an important part of our daily lives. Through writing skills we communicate our thoughts and feelings. We carry on education and business by writing.

"Perfect" handwriting should not be an end in itself. Handwriting is a skill that provides a means of expression. Ultimately, the focus of the student will be on the **message** rather than the handwriting per se. However, unless the message can be read by the receiver, it is worthless.

There are no shortcuts in learning to write legibly. It is a skill which cannot be picked up incidentally. Success is achieved only by consistent, daily practice. But when the proper conditions and environment support daily practice, the result will be measurable growth in handwriting skills.

Handwriting Time

A definite period for handwriting should be included in the daily schedule. About 10 minutes is a good length of time. After 10 minutes most students tire and lose efficiency.

A profitable time for handwriting is immediately following the opening exercises. Because of the content of *A Reason For Writing*, these lessons can naturally follow morning worship. The letters practiced in handwriting then become "special" letters for concentration or focus throughout the day.

Letter Formation

Naturally, it is vital for the teacher to be thoroughly familiar with all the letter forms used in *A Reason For Writing*. Even though it is similar to other writing methods, it is a distinctive writing style. Please take a few moments to refer to the charts on pages 45, 76, and 95. Since children tend to imitate the teacher in their handwriting, it is important to demonstrate the correct strokes for each letter before the students write it.

Typical Course of Study

KINDERGARTEN
1. Introduction of the letter sounds and symbols
2. Introduction of correct formation of the numerals 1-10
3. Introduction of letter stroke, including sequence and direction (formation of letters)
4. Instruction on holding a pencil and/or crayon correctly when writing

GRADE 1
1. Recognize and correctly form all letters of the alphabet and the numerals 1-10
2. Use the proper size for capital and lowercase letters
3. Hold a pencil correctly when printing
4. Practice good writing habits (e.g. posture, paper placement, pencil grip)

GRADE 2
1. Print all capital and lower case letters in proper form and size
2. Apply writing skills to all school assignments
3. Demonstrate awareness of proper writing formats (placement of writing on page)
4. Practice good writing habits (e.g. posture, paper placement, pencil grip)

GRADE 3
1. Write all letters in cursive writing
2. Write words in cursive writing with correct strokes (e.g. beginning, connecting and ending strokes)
3. Complete selected assignments in cursive writing
4. Use proper spacing between letters, words and sentences
5. Practice good writing habits (e.g. posture, paper placement, pencil grip)

GRADE 4
1. Write capital and lower-case cursive letters and words with proper form, size, slant, spacing and legibility
2. Use cursive writing to complete designated school assignments
3. Write with reasonable speed, a well-spaced paper with defined margins and indentations
4. Evaluate own handwriting to detect errors (slant, spacing, neatness)

GRADES 5-8
1. Write legibly using proper form, size, slant, and spacing
2. Write with rhythm and ease and without undue fatigue
3. Maintain printing skill for special purposes (e.g. maps, charts, posters, forms)
4. Teacher and student evaluate skills periodically to direct practice for improvement

Teaching
A Reason For Writing:

Introduction
To
Manuscript

God Made My World

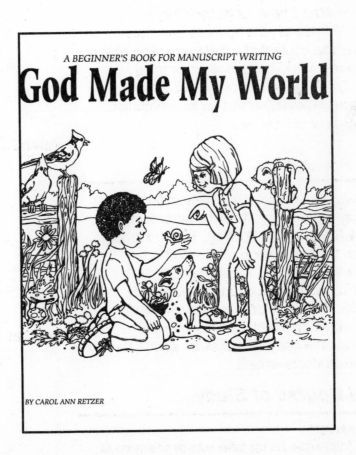

A BEGINNER'S BOOK FOR MANUSCRIPT WRITING

God Made My World

BY CAROL ANN RETZER

Manuscript Letter Formation

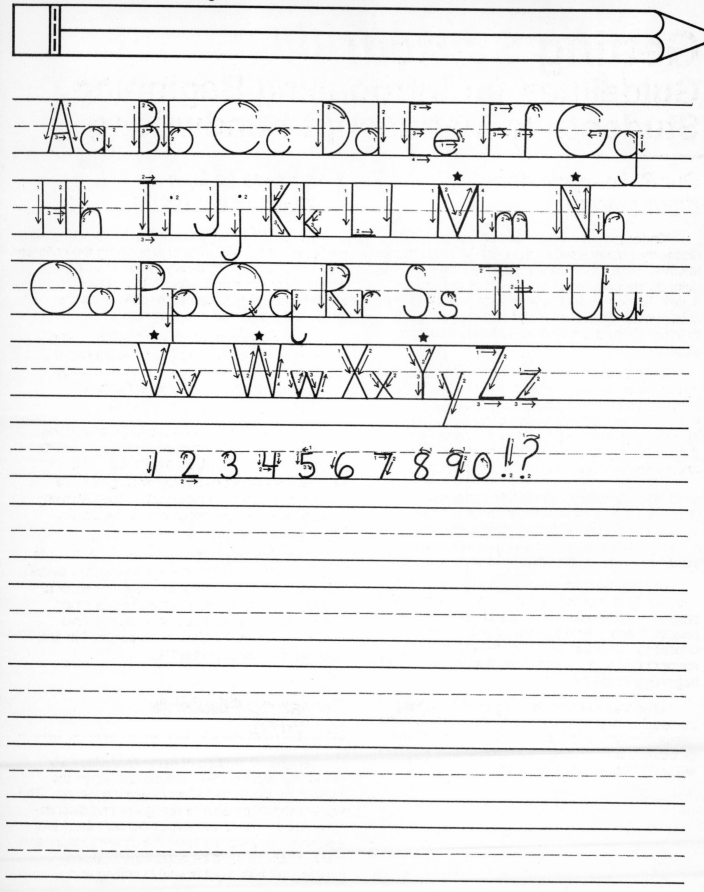

Getting Started:
Guidelines for Introducing Beginning Students to Manuscript Handwriting

Our Philosophy About Kindergarten

Kindergarten!—a year of beginning and discovery. Many issues face each kindergarten teacher. How much do we "push" a child? At what point do we encourage our students to read and write? Is there a measurable academic level each child should reach by the end of the year? Unfortunately, there are no simple answers that fit every situation.

Educators are recognizing that although many children can read and write at the age of four or five, pushing them in that direction may not be the best. If given a broader base of readiness and allowed to explore their world a bit longer, when they are ready they will quickly "pick up" reading and writing and soon catch up with their peers.

With this in mind, the readiness of each child—and each class—needs to be considered when planning the exciting year of kindergarten. A child's attitudes toward learning are set during these first months of school.

To help each child build a positive self-image, opportunity for success needs to be built into every program. As he sees the value of himself as a person, he can develop and grow in positive directions. Christian teachers in a caring environment can make a real difference in the lives of beginning students.

God Made My World is organized so that you, the teacher or parent, have options in meeting the needs of your student(s). Read the next section carefully and decide on an approach that you think will work best in your classroom.

Two Ways to Use "God Made My World"

The teacher may choose first to introduce all the letters of the alphabet before giving the children their copies of *God Made My World*. The introduction to God's world through the nature-enrichment activities can be expanded as the letters are introduced and taught.

With this method of introduction, using the Alphabet Wall Sheets (sold separately) is very helpful. The wall sheets can be colored and laminated for flashcards, or displayed around the classroom for a visual aid.

After all the letters have been presented and learned visually, students will begin writing in their copy of God Made My World. The teacher may choose to delay writing until the second semester of kindergarten, thus allowing more time for the development of the child's motor skills.

Another alternative is to let students write in their books as soon as the presentation of the alphabet is started. Introduce just one letter a day and don't push the children beyond their capabilities! The Alphabet Wall sheets and nature-enrichment activities will be used as the letter for the day is presented.

Preparing Students for Writing

Whichever method of using *God Made My World* you choose, there are certain things the student should know before beginning writing. The student should be able to recognize and discriminate among different letters of the alphabet. It is also necessary that he have the desire to write and that a dominant hand be established. Distinguishing left from right is vital in writing and reading. The teacher should continually stress the correct progression from left to right.

Activities that strengthen readiness for writing include:

- Cutting with scissors
- Drawing
- Working with clay
- Threading beads
- Using sewing cards
- Making designs with geometric shapes

Teach Correct Hand and Pencil Positions

The easiest time to teach students positioning is before they develop bad habits. Before handing out student books, teach the children the correct way to hold their pencils. Kindergarten children are eager to please, so capitalize on their eagerness and teach them correct position of their paper, pencil, and writing hand.

Encourage the student to hold the pencil between the thumb and index finger about half an inch above the sharpened part of the pencil. The middle finger will be used as a brace. The wrist needs to be relaxed so the hand can move easily for writing.

You may wish to say something like this, "You will want to hold your pencil this way (demonstrate) to make it easier for you to write." The teacher should keep his or her remarks as positive as possible. Look for a student who has correct positioning and praise him/her while encouraging others to form correct habits.

Although many books suggest that the paper be placed in a straight up-and-down position on the desk, most children find it easier to write when the paper is slanted slightly, about the same as the slant of the writing arm.

The student's desk and seat need to be at the correct height. A child should be able to sit up straight with both feet flat on the floor. His forearms

Paper placement for a right-handed student.

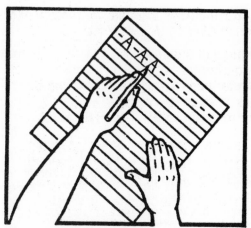

Paper placement for a left-handed student.

should rest on the desk. The chair should be close enough to the desk so that the child does not have to bend forward too much. Before introducing the handwriting lesson, make sure any unnecessary materials are cleared from each student's desk.

How To Form Manuscript Letters

Most manuscript letters are made without lifting the pencil. The exceptions are the k, x, y, and of course the i, j, f, and t which have a dot or a cross added after the rest of the letter is formed.

This continuous-line formation will allow for much easier carry over to cursive writing. It is difficult for arrows to indicate adequately the formation of the letter and the movement of the pencil. Just remember that most letters will be written without the pencil being lifted from the paper. Stress that most letters are started at the top.

Many kindergarten students begin writing in all capital letters. This should be discouraged because it is a difficult habit to break. In this book the lowercase letters are introduced first, because they are used most frequently in writing.

Of course, students will need capital letters for the beginning of their names. Show each one how to correctly make the letter for his or her name.

What's Included in "God Made My World"?

God Made My World begins with readiness circles and lines, then introduces each lowercase letter before adding capital letters. Review lessons are included throughout the book to help maintain the letters already covered.

This manual includes the following information for each lesson in *God Made My World:*

● The formation of the letter
● The sound(s) of the letter
● Directions for completing the work page on the back of each letter page.
● Resource material on the object pictured

The "key picture" for each letter is intended to give the student a visual tie between the letter and its sound. Basic resource material about each nature "key picture" in *God Made My World* is included in this *Teachers Instruction Guidebook.*

The teacher may wish to check the school or public library for additional information on the nature topics. Hands-on material will help to reinforce in the child's mind the link between the object, the letter, and the sound—so include as much as possible.

A student needs a definite mental image of a letter—as well as the strokes needed to form it—in order to write it correctly. If he has an incorrect perception of the letter, he will probably not write it correctly. So it's vital that enough readiness activities are provided so that students will accurately perceive each letter. The next section includes a number of suggestions for introducing each letter of the alphabet.

How to Introduce New Letters

1. Describe the sound.

2. Name the letter.

3. Describe the strokes and demonstrate how the letter is made.

4. Use the chalkboard or overhead projector to demonstrate how the letter is made.

5. Sky write the letter. Using the pointer finger of the writing hand, outline the letter in the air slightly above eye level. Say the letter sound or describe the strokes as you sky write the letter. Children should imitate the teacher's movements as closely as possible.

6. Palm write the letter. Using the pointer finger of the writing hand, outline the letter on the opposite palm, describing it aloud as it is formed.

7. Write the letter in finger paints (if there is time and/or the student needs more tactile experience).

8. Write the letter in sand or a shallow box filled with salt or cornmeal.

The teaching sequence for maximum student benefit should be:

● **See** the letter.

● **Hear** the letter. Hear the name of the letter, the sound(s) it makes, and a description of the strokes used in forming the letter. (See page 14 for a more detailed teaching plan.)

● **Move** with the shape of the letter.

● Finally **write** the letter on paper.

The Left-Handed Child

Don't let a left-handed student use an exaggerated or hooked arm or paper position! Habits that will last a lifetime are established in the kindergarten classroom, and many left-handed students will need the teacher's special encouragement and patience as they learn the basics of writing.

The left-handed child should be encouraged to do the outlined exercises using his left hand as the writing hand. The left-handed paper and pencil positions are the same relaxed position as the right-handed positions. The paper should follow the slant of the arm.

Special Helps

Two sections in each day's teaching outline deserve the teacher's special attention. The first gives basic information about the object to be studied. In some cases the teacher will need to prepare additional visual aids. This may be checking out a butterfly book from the library or finding colored pictures of birds' nests.

Several suggestions are given for the "Work Page," the back side of the lesson page. For some of these activities the teacher will need to prepare and set out yarn, glue, construction paper, glitter, etc.

Introductory Pages

The first few pages of the book are to acquaint the student with the concepts of letter formation— following the direction of arrows, making the downstrokes, and tracing the dotted lines.

PAGE 5

This book frequently uses dotted lines. The first page gives the student practice in following a dotted line. Holding the pencil as directed, the student should be instructed to follow the line from the rabbit to the carrot, the giraffe to the leaf, and the bee to the flowers.

If the student has difficulty following the dotted line, he or she may not be ready for writing. It may be appropriate to delay writing a few more weeks. Instead, let the student do more painting, stringing of beads, and other pre-writing activities.

PAGE 6

Circles are used in forming many letters of the manuscript alphabet. Many letters are made using the counter-clockwise stroke. Let the student choose a green, red, or purple crayon to trace the grapes. Watch to make sure he/she is following the direction of the arrows.

After the grapes are correctly traced, encourage the student to finish coloring the picture. If the student needs more practice making circles in the right direction, ask him/her to draw another bunch of grapes on a large sheet of plain paper.

PAGE 7

Before letting the students trace the bubbles in their books, blow some real bubbles in the classroom. Children love the bubble kits that can be purchased at a variety or drug store. Let them enjoy the beautiful colors and shapes as they blow bubbles.

Next move into sky writing. You can do this with one or two students or have the entire class practice together drawing circles in the air. Emphasize the counter-clockwise formation.

After a few minutes of bubble-blowing and sky writing, instruct the students to trace the bubbles in their books, emphasizing again the proper counter-clockwise formation. Let the students choose varied colored crayons to use as they trace in their books. They can finish the page by coloring the girl.

Allowing students extra practice on the chalkboard will make any stroke direction problem easy for the teacher to spot.

PAGE 8

The most common line stroke in letter formation is the down stroke. Emphasize the top to bottom stroke. Discuss with the class straight lines they can see around the classroom—walls, edges of tables, desks, windows, etc.

Explain that there are many straight lines in writing, too. Introduce this stroke to the students and ask them to follow the arrows as they trace each line.

To conclude the lesson on straight lines, ask each student to draw a picture on a separate sheet of paper **using only straight lines.** Suggest a simple house, a picture frame, a skyscraper, etc. Students may find a ruler helpful in this exercise. Share pictures when each student has finished.

PAGE 9

Take a "circle walk" around the school. The students look for objects that are circles as they become more aware of the shapes in their world. Discuss the objects as you walk.

They may spot objects such as these: clocks, balls, lights, etc. After the circle walk, students can trace the large and small circles. (At this point don't refer to them as "capital" and "lowercase" O's. The students are still practicing strokes they will use in making letters.) To conclude the lesson, have the children draw pictures of the "circle" objects they have seen.

PAGE 10

Students will alternate between circles and straight lines on this page. Make sure they are following the arrows as they trace the patterns and then make their own shapes.

For an art project, suggest that each student draw a picture using only straight lines and circles. (Suggest a baseball and bat, a bicycle, and a watch.) Let the students talk about the finished pictures.

PAGE 11

Talk about straight lines that are diagonal. Draw a simple teepee on the chalkboard. Explain that several letters of the alphabet use slant (diagonal) lines. Let the students trace the patterns on the page.

What kind of pictures can students draw using slant lines? How about an ice cream cone, a tent, the roof of a house? See if each student can come up with a different shape to draw and color.

PAGE 12

This is the last practice page before beginning the alphabet, so the circles are smaller. Watch each student as he traces the bubbles to make sure he is forming the circle in a counter-clockwise direction.

If any student is having a problem with direction, now is the time to catch it! Correct formation is **so** important, so give any student with problems the help necessary before beginning the alphabet.

Encourage the students to color the fish with bright-colored crayons. If they wish, students can add seashells, seaweed, or other fish to their picture. (If available, let students glue small shells to the page!)

Beginning the Alphabet

The letters in this book are not introduced in alphabetical order. Instead, they are presented by groups made with similar strokes. This should help the student to master the strokes as they are presented and give a feeling of success.

The strokes used in each letter should be verbalized and demonstrated before the student takes up his pencil to write. It is difficult for children to visualize the symbol (letter) unless they can picture the way it is made.

You will need to be involved in individual supervision as your students begin to write. Circulate around the room as much as possible. Praise for correct formation and encouragement will aid the students' success. Be patient and persistent as you present each letter!

Correct letter formation cannot be emphasized too much! It is difficult to correct a child who has learned incorrect habits of formation, so try to prevent your students from developing poor writing habits. If a student needs more practice, use the black-line master on page 41 to provide lines like the student's workbook for practice.

Teaching Plan for Each Letter

The following information is included for each lesson:

● **A description of the way the letter is formed.** The directions for each lesson page are the same (so they are not repeated for each letter). "Trace the letter in the tree house, following the arrows. Then finish writing the letters on the page."

● **The sound(s) of the letter, as used in common words.** Depending upon your phonics program, you may decide to introduce only one sound for each letter—the sound for the beginning of the key picture. However, additional sounds are also included in the teaching plan.

● **Background information about the "key picture."** This can be supplemented with information from other sources.

● **Instructions for completing a project with the picture side of the lesson.**

Much information in the teaching plan is included in quotation marks so the teacher has the option of using it exactly as it is written. Of course many teachers will adapt it to their own style, but those who prefer to read directly from this manual will have all the information needed.

How the Tree House Can Help in Letter Positioning

The concept of the tree house is helpful in explaining to beginning writers the position of lowercase letters in relation to the lines. The tree house is used through the lowercase section of *God Made My World.*

Explain that the main part of the letter is written within the area of the tree house. Some letters begin at the top of the roof; others begin in the meeting room; and still others begin in the meeting room and go down the ladder to the ground.

Students will grasp the concept of the new letter more quickly if you say, "The **b** begins at the roof and goes to the bottom of the meeting room" or "Shouldn't your **g** go clear down to the ground?"

You may wish to draw a tree house on an overhead transparency master or the chalkboard and demonstrate each new letter in the tree house as part of the introduction.

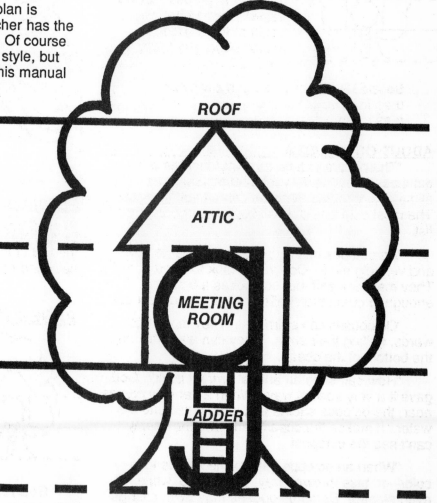

Lowercase Letters:
Specific Instructions for Teaching Lowercase Manuscript Letters

PAGES 13 & 14—o

[Teacher: Introduce each letter by writing it on the chalkboard and sky writing it. To help them internalize the letter's formation, have students join you in sky writing the letter.]

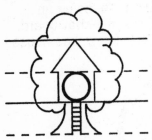

Description of letter: "This is the letter **o**. It is made exactly like the bubbles that we drew in the air and the grapes that we traced. Remember, we begin at the 2 o'clock position and go up and around."

Sounds of letter: **o** as in **octopus**.
o as in **orange**.
o as in **do**.

ABOUT OCTOPUSES

"The picture to help us remember the **o** is the octopus. They are very interesting creatures. They all have eight arms, but they come in different sizes. The most common size is about as large as a man's fist.

"An octopus has a round body, a large head, and very big eyes. Octopuses look for food at night. They may look soft, but octopuses are strong enough to crush the shells of other sea creatures!

"Octopuses can swim fast. They move backwards, trailing their arms. They can also walk on the bottom of the ocean.

"How can such an animal protect itself? God gave it a very special way. When an enemy comes near, the octopus squirts a colored liquid into the water. It makes the ocean dark, and the enemy can't see the octopus!

"When an octopus gets excited it changes color—to blue, brown, gray, purple, red, white, or even striped! Some octopuses may even change color to hide in their surroundings. This is a very interesting sea creature that God has made."

Consult your encyclopedia for pictures of octopuses. *The How and Why Wonder Book of*

Sea Shells, published by Grossett and Dunlap, has simple explanations of many seashells and sea animals. Look for it in your library. Expand the explanation of the octopus as far as interest holds.

OCTOPUS WORK PAGE

"Decide what color you want your octopus to be and color it. Outline the octopus carefully first, then fill in the lines. Color in some ocean water and seaweed so the octopus can swim around."

PAGES 15 & 16—c

Description of letter: "This is the letter **c**. It fills the tree house but does not complete the circle. Remember to start at the 2 o'clock position. Like a sleepy cat, this letter curls up and around. But don't go all the way around like a bubble!"

Sounds of letter: **c** as in **cat**. [Say the sound as you write it on the chalkboard and in the air.]
c as in **cedar**.

15

ABOUT CATS

Share with the students a picture book about cats. Encourage them to tell about their own cats—name, color, size, favorite habit, etc.

CAT WORK PAGE

"Color the cat the color you would like your own cat to be. Then design and color a nice warm rug for the cat to rest on."

PAGES 17 & 18—g

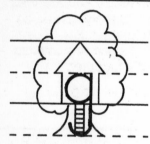

Description of letter:
"Look at the way the letter **g** sits in the tree house. At the foot of the ladder it curls around like a monkey's tail. Begin the letter **g** at the 2 o'clock position, go up and around, then bring the stem and tail down and around without picking up your pencil."

Sounds of letter: g as in **goose**.
g as in **giraffe**.

ABOUT GEESE

"What animals do you know that look a lot like a goose? (ducks and swans). They all have webbed feet that make them good swimmers. Geese are larger than most ducks, but smaller than swans. They are pretty creatures, aren't they?

"Geese eat grains and vegetables. Once in awhile they also eat insects and small water creatures.

"Geese live as long as 30 years. A pair of geese stay together for life! The female goose makes a nest in a hollow of the ground. God made this animal to know to make her nest soft. She lines it with soft feathers from her breast and then lays 3 to 6 white eggs.

"A male goose is called a *gander*. Ganders are good fathers. They help the mother while the babies are being hatched and raised."

GOOSE WORK PAGE

"Many geese are white, so you may choose to leave yours uncolored. But the Canada Goose is grayish-brown, and its head, neck, and tail are black, and its underparts gray. You may wish to color your picture like a Canada Goose.

"Color the goose's beak orange. The feet and eyes should be black.

"Canada Geese lay from 5 to 9 pale green, yellowish, or off-white eggs. Other geese lay white eggs.

"Draw a nest with eggs in it. Make sure the eggs in your nest match the kind of goose you have colored. The goose would probably find a nice grassy place to build her nest, so add some grass around your goose's nest."

PAGES 19 & 20—q

Description of letter:
"The letter **q** is similar to the letter **g**, except the tail curls in the other direction." [Make **q**'s in the air and on the chalkboard. Describe the motions as you make the letter for the students to see.] "Start at the 2 o'clock position, go up and around, down and to the **right**."

Sound of letter: q as in **quail**.

ABOUT QUAIL

"Quail are pretty little birds. Have you ever seen a quail running across the road with its family? A quail family has an interesting name: a *covey*. There may be as many as 18 babies in a covey!

"God gave quail a good way to protect them - selves. They have speckled brown feathers so they can hide easily in bushes and grasses. When they stay very still, it's hard to see them hiding."

QUAIL WORK PAGE
"Design a speckled look for your quail. Then draw a bush and some grass for the quail to hide in. Can you find a feather to glue on the quail?"

PAGES 21 & 22—s

Description of letter:
"This is the letter **s**. It just curves around." [Make the sound as you draw the letter in the air. Then draw it in your hand. Have each child follow your motions and draw it in his/her hand.]

Sounds of letter: s as in **snail**.

ABOUT SNAILS
"A snail is very interesting because it carries its house on its back! The snail's house—or shell—looks like a coiled seashell.

"You might find a snail in a damp, shady place, like a garden. The snail creeps along on one foot. It will stick out a body and show its head with feelers, eyes, and a mouth with tiny teeth.

"Some snails have quite colorful shells. But plain garden snails are usually brown."

SNAIL WORK PAGE
"Color your snail with crayons. Then glue yarn on the coil of its shell."

PAGES 23 & 24—d

Description of letter:
"The letter **d** begins like the letter **c**, then goes all the way to the top of the tree house and back to the floor again." [Say the sound as you make the letter. Then say, "Let's practice making some **d**'s together."]

Sound of the letter: d as in **dog**.

ABOUT DOGS
"There are so many kinds of dogs—big dogs, little dogs, dogs with long tails, dogs with almost no tails. Dogs come in many colors and with different types of fur."

Try to find a book with pictures of several kinds of dogs. Share dog stories.

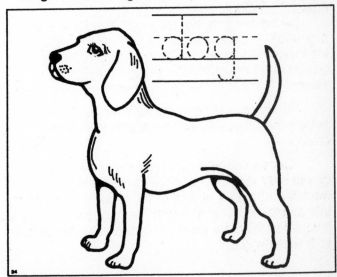

DOG WORK PAGE

"Color the dog to look like your dog. If you don't own a dog, color the picture to look like a dog you would like to have. Do you think the dog needs a toy? Design and color something a dog likes to play with or chew on." [Suggest a ball, stick, rubber chew, bone, etc.]

PAGES 25 & 26—Review

This is the first review page. Others will follow the same pattern. Before the students take up their pencils, sky write each letter and review the formation of each letter.

Tell the children to draw a line from the picture to the letter that starts the name of that creature. Then the students should write three or four letters to fill the line.

If any student is having trouble, take time now to review with him the letters covered so far.

PAGES 27 & 28—a

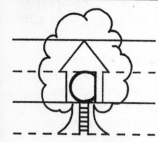

Description of letter:
"The letter **a** begins like an **o** but has a line added to the side. Don't pick up your pencil until you have made the whole letter!"

Sounds of letter: **a** as in **apple**.

a as in **ape**.

a as in **want** (ah).

ABOUT APPLES

"Apples come in several colors. Can you tell me what they are? [red, yellow, green]

"Help me describe an apple. [peeling on outside, white inside, crunchy, seeds in the middle, stem, etc.]

"God made something special inside each apple. Did you know there's a star inside? Let's cut one open and see. [Cut through the round part—the "equator"—and the seed section should show a star shape.]

"How many seeds do you think are in an apple?" [Compare at least three apples to see if there are the same number of seeds in each.]

At lunchtime, taste apples of different colors to see which the students like best.

APPLE WORK PAGE

"Outline the picture of the apple carefully in the color of apple you like best. When you have finished coloring the picture, glue two apple seeds in the right place."

PAGES 29 & 30—b

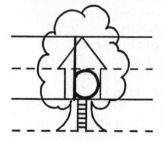

Description of letter:
"Begin the **b** at the roof of the tree house and end at the floor. With your pencil go down-up-and-circle-around, without lifting your pencil."

Sound of letter: **b** as in **bear**.

ABOUT BEARS

"When you hear the word **bear**, what comes to your mind first? Smokey the Bear? A teddy bear? A white polar bear?

"Real bears look friendly, but they can be very dangerous in the wild. Bears have small eyes and they can't see very well. But they have a very good sense of smell.

"Bears spend the winter sleeping. This deep sleep is called *hibernation*. How do they know when to go to sleep? God must make them sleepy. Just before they go into hibernation they eat enough food to keep them alive for several months.

"While she is hibernating, the female bear may give birth to one or two cubs. They are very tiny! When spring comes, the cubs start growing fast.

"Even though bears can be dangerous, they are peace-loving. They try to keep out of fights and will run from danger. Perhaps we should be more like the bears."

BEAR WORK PAGE

"Color your bear either dark brown or black. This bear looks as if he smells something good to eat. Do you know something bears like to eat? Honey! Would you like to draw a jar of honey for the bear to eat?"

PAGES 31 & 32—p

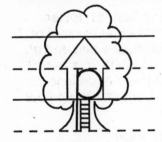

Description of letter: "The letter **p** starts at the dotted line of the tree house. Go down the ladder to the ground, then back up and make a circle in the meeting room. Don't lift your pencil until you've finished the whole letter!"

Sound of letter: p as in **pumpkin**. [Make sure students are not making a **pu** sound. Here's a way to check what they are saying. "Hold a tissue in front on your mouth. If you make the **p** sound correctly, a slight breeze from your mouth will move the tissue."]

ABOUT PUMPKINS

"Pumpkins are large and round and orange. How do you eat pumpkin? Maybe in a pumpkin pie? There's another part of the pumpkin you can also eat."

If you can get a pumpkin to take to class, cut it open to show the children the stringy inside. Carefully remove the seeds and wash them.

Let the students count the seeds into paper cups, each containing 10 seeds. Then stack the cups into groups of hundreds, tens, and ones to see how many seeds are in the pumpkin.

After counting the seeds, wash them again and soak them in salty water. Spread them on a cookie sheet and roast them in a warm oven (250°) for 45-

60 minutes. The seeds will puff up a bit as they roast. Enjoy cracking the roasted pumpkin seeds at lunch time. This may be a new taste adventure for your students!

PUMPKIN WORK PAGE

"Outline the pumpkin with your orange crayon. Color the pumpkin with smooth strokes. Finish with a green stem and leaf.

"Some people make jack-o-lanterns out of pumpkins by drawing or cutting faces on them. Would you like to make your pumpkin into a jack-o-lantern? If you decide to, make it a happy face! Triangle shapes make good eyes and noses for jack-o-lanterns."

PAGES 33 & 34—r

Description of letter: "The letter **r** is a short letter that does not go above or below the dotted line. Start at the dotted line and go down to the solid line, then back up to the same line and round it off to the 2 o'clock position."

Sound of letter: r as in **rainbow**. [The mouth should be rounded. Be careful not to say **er**.]

ABOUT RAINBOWS

"The rainbow is in an *arc* shape. Doesn't it remind you of the arc on the letter **r**?

"Can you think of all the colors in the rain-bow?" [violet, blue, green, yellow, orange, and red].

"We see rainbows when the sun is behind us and the rain is in front of us. Have you ever seen a rainbow in the garden hose? Early some morning (or late in the afternoon) ask your parents to help you make a rainbow in your yard! With your back to the sun, spray the water into a dark background.

such as a tree or building. The water droplets will form a rainbow!

"Be watching to see rainbows other places, too.

"There's a favorite rainbow story in the Bible. Do you remember the story of the very first rainbow?" [Gen. 9:12-17]

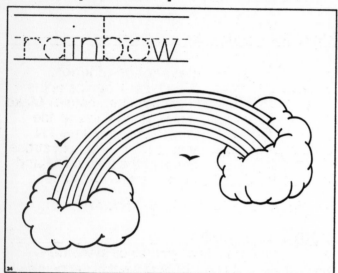

RAINBOW WORK PAGE

Let the children use water colors to paint their rainbow picture. The water colors will blend slightly and give the picture a soft look. Review the order of the colors.

Making a rainbow book is a fun activity for individual students to work on or to plan together as a group project. It's especially fun to do on a rainy day!

Plan a page for each color of the rainbow. Let the children look through old magazines or picture files to find pictures of things that are red, blue, yellow, etc. Have them paste each picture on the correct page. If possible, color-coordinate the pages on contruction paper. Or write the word in the color it names.

Punch holes in the pages and tie them together with yarn or fasten them with rings. Make a cover that says "My [Our] Rainbow Book."

PAGES 35 & 36—m

Description of letter: "The letter **m** is like a hill with two humps. Start at the dotted line and go down to the solid line, then back up, making the first hump, and down, up, hump, down. Isn't that fun to make?"

Sound of letter: m as in **moon**. "Do you feel your lips tingle when you make the sound?"

ABOUT THE MOON

"The moon is the brightest thing you will see in the sky at night. Have you seen the moon look as if it were shaped differently at various times of the month? It doesn't really change shape, but differents parts of it are lighted by the sun as it goes around the earth. Watch for the different shapes."

Check out the phase of the moon the day before presenting this lesson and tell your students what shape they can expect to see if they look in the sky the night after you talk about the moon.

MOON WORK PAGE

"Color your moon yellow. Do you have a silver crayon for coloring the stars? If not, make them light yellow. Carefully make the sky black or dark blue. Would you like to add some star stickers to make your picture even prettier?"

PAGES 37 & 38—n

Description of letter:
"The letter **n** is made like the letter **m**, but it has only one hump. Start at the dotted line, go down, up, hump, and down to the solid line."

Sound of letter: n as in **nest**.

ABOUT NESTS

"It's fun to find a bird's nest in a tree or bush! It's even more exciting if the nest has eggs or baby birds in it.

"Most birds build nests to hold their eggs and shelter their young. Nests can be just a few stones or bits of grass by the water (for water birds) or a hole inside a tree (for a woodpecker). Other birds build nests out of mud and straw. The most common building materials for nests are straw, twigs, and feathers."

From an encyclopedia or bird book, show the children colored photographs or drawings of several kinds of nests. Tell them which bird makes which nest, and talk about birds that live in your area of the country.

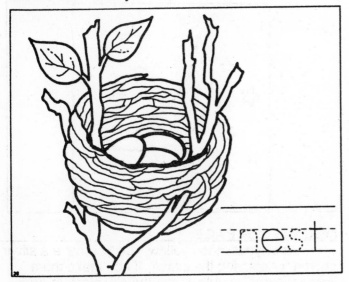

NEST WORK PAGE

"Did you see a picture of a nest you'd like to make? Color your picture to make it look like the nest of a bird that might live in your neighborhood. Make sure the eggs are the right kind for your nest." [For example, mockingbird eggs are speckled, and robin eggs are pale blue.] "Can you draw the bird that would build that nest?"

PAGES 39 & 40—Review

Take time to review the sound of each of the six letters just studied. With sky writing and on the chalkboard review how each is formed. Circulate around the classroom to make sure each student has thoroughly mastered the letters before beginning the next section.

PAGES 41 & 42—k

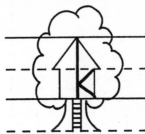

Description of letter:
"The letter **k** begins at the roof of the tree house. Make a nice straight line all the way to the solid line. Lift your pencil. The next stroke starts at the dotted line and goes slant in, slant out".

Sound of letter: k as in **kangaroo**.

ABOUT KANGAROOS

"What makes a kangaroo so different from other animals? Its pouch! And what is the pouch used for?

"Baby kangaroos, called *joeys*, are as tiny as baby mice when they are born. They stay nice and cozy in their mother's pouch for several weeks. Finally the joeys are old enough to bounce outside part of the day. But they jump back inside the warm pouch at night!"

KANGAROO WORK PAGE

"Kangaroos are usually either reddish brown or gray. Choose one of these colors to make your kangaroo mother and joey. Would you like to draw a second joey who is not riding in the pouch with his sister? He should be the same color as his mother and sister, shouldn't he?"

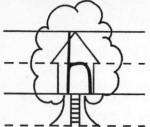

Description of letter:
"The letter **h** looks a lot like a chair. Begin it at the roof of the tree house. Go straight down, then up and over."

Sound of letter: h as in **hippo**. ["Hold your hand close to your mouth and say the sound. Do you feel little puffs of air warming your hand?"]

ABOUT HIPPOS

"The hippo is one of the biggest land animals. Doesn't he look clumsy? Did you know that a hippo can run as fast as a person? He's also a very good swimmer!

"Have you seen a hippo in the zoo? The main place hippos live is in Africa. They usually spend most of their lives near rivers. Many hours of a hippo day are spent in the water. If you ever see one swimming, you may see only his little ears and eyes above the water!

"A baby hippo is called a *calf*. A hippo calf often rides on its mother's back in the water."

HIPPO WORK PAGE

"A hippo has thick, brownish-gray skin. Color your mother hippo that color. Can you draw a calf on her back?"

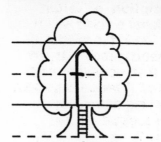

Description of letter:
"The letter **f** is a tall letter. It starts in the attic, curves up and around, then goes straight down like a cane. Lift your pencil and make a cross mark at the dotted line. Make sure you draw the cross from left to right!"

Sound of letter: f as in **frog**. ["Do you feel air escaping between your teeth and lip as you make the **f** sound?"]

ABOUT FROGS

"How do frogs move? They hop or leap with their long back legs. Many frogs can leap as much as 20 times their body length on a level surface!

"Frogs spend part of their lives on land and part in the water. Their long, strong legs make them good swimmers.

"God gave frogs special eyes. They bulge out, which may look funny to you, but it helps Mr. Frog see in almost any direction. Why is this important? So the frog can see insects anywhere near him. When a bug comes close—zap! Mr. Frog scoops him up with his long tongue. Frogs eat a lot of insects that would be pests to us.

"During recess today we'll play a game called Leapfrog."

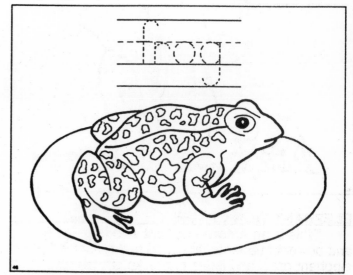

FROG WORK PAGE

"Frogs often blend in with their surroundings. This frog is green, like the lily pad he's sitting on. Color them both green. If you have two green crayons, make the frog darker. Then color the pond blue with blue crayons or water colors."

PAGES 47 & 48—e

Description of letter:
"The letter **e** starts with a short line in the middle of the meeting room—to the right, then up and around like a **c**." [Demonstrate with sky writing as you say, "Across, circle up, and around."]

Sounds of letter: e as in **elephant**.

e as in **east**.

ABOUT ELEPHANTS

"The elephant is the largest land animal. Have you seen an elephant in the circus or the zoo? Don't they look interesting with their wrinkled gray skin?

"God made a wonderful tool for the elephant. Can you guess what it is? The trunk! An elephant's trunk may be six feet long. He can push over a small tree with it—or pick up a single leaf!

"Elephants eat plants. One elephant may eat as much as 300 pounds of food a day! Don't let one in your refrigerator!"

ELEPHANT WORK PAGE

"This is an African elephant with large ears and powerful upper teeth called *tusks*. Color the elephant gray, and leave the tusks uncolored. Perhaps you'd like to draw a peanut near the elephant's trunk. Wouldn't that be a nice snack for him to pick up in his trunk?" (Or students could eat peanuts and glue a shell to their elephant sheets.)

PAGES 49 & 50—i

Description of letter:
"The letter **i** is simple to make! Just start at the dotted line and make a straight line to the floor. Then pick up your pencil and put a small dot in the middle of the space."

Sounds of letter: i as in **insect**.

i as in **I**. ["Think of the name you sometimes call yourself."]

ABOUT INSECTS

"This insect looks like a bee. Bees live in groups called *colonies*. Their home is called a *hive*.

"Each member of the colony has a special job to do. Some bees get food. The queen lays eggs. Others protect the colony from danger. Isn't it wonderful that such tiny insects can work together so well?

"The bee is the only insect that makes something that we eat. Do you know what it is? Bees make honey in a honeycomb." [Try to find a honeycomb to show the students at this point.]

"Bees help farmers, too. As they go from flower to flower getting nectar to make honey, tiny bits of *pollen* stick to them. This pollen makes the the other plants grow better.

"There are many other insects. You may want to collect some and find their names in a book."

INSECT WORK PAGE

"The body of a bee is black and yellow. The wings are *transparent*, which means you can see through them. Color the eyes and legs black.

"Cut some pictures of flowers out of a magazine, or make your own from construction paper, or add flower stickers to your page. Bees like lots of flowers, so have fun filling your insect page!

"Maybe you'd like to eat a butter-and-honey sandwich at lunchtime to remind you of the helpful bee."

PAGES 51 & 52—j

Description of letter: "The letter **j** begins like the **i** but goes down the ladder to the ground and curves up like a monkey tail. When you have finished the letter, pick up your pencil and place a small dot on the middle of the top space."

Sound of letter: j as in **jonquil**.

ABOUT JONQUILS

[Have a jonquil bulb in your hand.] "Do you know what this is? No, it's not an onion. It doesn't look much like a flower, does it? But it will some - day!

"A bulb is a bud that lives underground to keep the flower alive during the winter. It has food stored in it.

"As spring comes and the weather gets warmer, the plant begins to come up through the soil. We'll plant this bulb and watch it grow! Someday it will look like this." [Show silk or real flower.]

"Can you think of other flowers that grow from bulbs?" [tulips, daffodils, narcissus, etc.]

JONQUIL WORK PAGE
"Color the trumpet of your jonquil light yellow. The back petals should be darker yellow. The stem and leaves are green. Color the pot any color you like."

PAGES 53 & 54—Review
Circulate around the classroom as the students work on these review pages. Make sure each child can make all six letters correctly before moving on to the next lesson.

PAGES 55 & 56—l

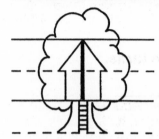

Description of letter: "The letter **l** is an easy letter to make. Just start at the roof of the tree house and make a straight line down to the floor. Make sure you begin at the top and come down!"

Sound of letter: l as in **lion**.

ABOUT LIONS
"A lion is a great big cat. But the lion is very fierce and has a loud roar. The lion is called *the king of beasts*.

"The picture in your book shows a male lion. How can you tell? See the ruff of fur around his head? It's called a *mane*. The male lion is the only cat with a mane. It makes him look even bigger and stronger!

"Lions live in a group called a *pride*. If one lion in the pride has been away, when he comes back the other lions rub his cheeks in greeting. How can you greet your friends with Christian love?"

LION WORK PAGE
"Color the body and face of your lion tawny gold. Make his eyes green. To make a fluffy mane

for your lion, cut pieces of yarn and glue them to your picture. Isn't he a handsome beast? Can you see why he is called *the king of beasts*?"

PAGES 57 & 58—t

Description of letter:
"The letter **t** begins in the middle of the attic and comes straight down. Pick up your pencil and make a small cross mark on the dotted line, going from left to right."

Sound of letter: t as in **turtle**.

ABOUT TURTLES

"God gave the turtle a wonderful way to protect himself. When he senses danger, he just pulls his head, legs, and tail safely inside the shell covering his back!

"The female turtle digs a hole in the ground and lays eggs. Then she covers the eggs and goes away. The sun keeps the eggs nice and warm, and they soon hatch into baby turtles. The babies never see their mother.

"Do you know anything about the way turtles move? We think of turtles as moving slowly but steadily. However, in water a turtle can swim fast.

"Turtles come in many colors and sizes. Some are plain black, brown, or dark green. Others are bright green, orange, red, or yellow. Some have bright spots of color on dark bodies and shells."

TURTLE WORK PAGE

"Choose the color or colors you want your turtle to be. Then draw some plants for the turtle to munch on."

PAGES 59 & 60—u

Description of letter:
"The letter **u** begins at the dotted line, goes down, and curves right back up to the line, finishing with a straight line down. Don't lift your pencil until you've finished the letter!"

Sounds of letter: u as in **universe**.

u as in **umbrella** (the most common).

ABOUT THE UNIVERSE

"God made the whole *universe*. The universe includes the earth and everything on it, and everything we can see in the sky. The universe is so big nobody knows its real size!

"But even in this huge universe, God knows about each person in it. Isn't it wonderful that He cares about you and me?

"Would you like to learn the names of the planets? Going out from the sun they are [in order]: Mercury, Venus, Earth, Mars, Jupiter, Saturn, Uranus, Neptune, and Pluto."

UNIVERSE WORK PAGE

"Can you see Earth in this picture of the universe? Color the oceans blue and the land either brown or green. What color should the stars be?

"You are a part of the universe. Draw your smiling face on this page to remind you that you are part of God's universe. You may also want to draw your family and friends too. Put as many faces as you can around the universe."

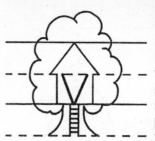

Description of letter: "In making the letter **y**, you lift your pencil once. Start with a slanting line from the dotted line to the floor. Lift your pencil and make another slanting one that goes down the ladder to the ground. Isn't that easy?"

Sound of letter: y as in **yak**. ["Has your mother ever said you 'yak' too much? But today we're talking about the animal named yak."]

ABOUT YAKS

"The yak lives is a far-away country called Tibet. Tibet has very high mountains, and the yak is a useful animal to the people who live there.

"The yak is a pack animal—it carries heavy loads. People and mail travel on yaks in places cars can't go.

"The yak also gives milk in a country where there are no cows. Even the soft hair of the yak is used to make warm coats.

"Does it look like the yak would move slowly? Don't be fooled! A yak can slide down icy slopes and swim swift-running rivers. Look for a yak the next time you go to a zoo."

YAK WORK PAGE

"Color your yak black or dark brown. Give her black hooves. Because a yak has soft hair, glue short pieces of dark yarn over the shaggy coat of your yak."

Description of letter: "The letter **v** is a fun letter to make. Start at the dotted line and make a slant line to the solid line, then another slant line going up. Make sure you don't pick up your pencil until you've finished the letter!"

Sound of letter: v as in **vegetables**. ["Put your hand close to your mouth. As you say the sound, do you feel a little air coming out between your lips?"]

ABOUT VEGETABLES

With a little advanced preparation, you can have a very interesting lesson on vegetables. The day before, ask each student to bring one vegetable to school the next day. Suggest carrots, celery, onions, broccoli, turnips, potatoes, cauliflower, etc.

To make Classroom Vegetable Soup, you will need to have a slow cooker, seasonings, sharp knives, a stirring spoon, and paper bowls and plastic spoons ready. Plan the lesson for early in the day. Then get your vegetable soup simmering in the slow cooker. You may wish to practice at home to see how long your slow cooker takes to cook vegetable soup.

"There are so many different kinds of vegetables! See all the ones we've brought today!

"We eat the roots of some vegetables, like turnips, carrots, potatoes, and onions. We eat the celery and broccoli and cauliflower plants themselves.

"We eat what other vegetable plants produce: peas, squash, and peppers.

"Let's try a tiny taste of some vegetables raw before we put them into our soup. Do you like the taste of raw potato? carrot? pepper?"

If you have a teacher's aide, let her prepare the vegetables and start the soup cooking. If possible, keep the slow cooker where the children can see it. Enjoy your Classroom Vegetable Soup at lunchtime!

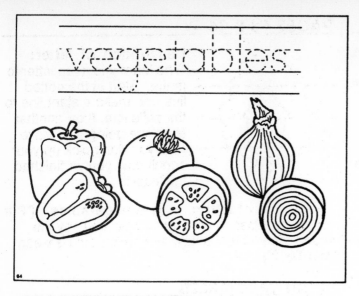

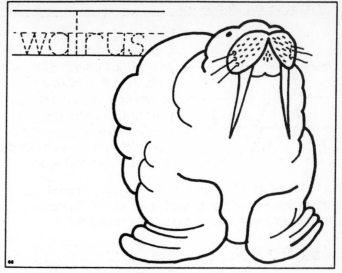

VEGETABLE WORK PAGE

"Vegetables come in such pretty colors! You can color the pepper red, green, or yellow. The tomato should be bright red. What about the onion? It could be brown, white, or purple-red."

"Why don't you draw pictures of two more vegetables you especially like?"

PAGES 65 & 66—w

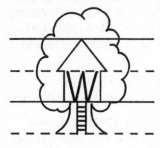

Description of letter: "The letter **w** is made like two **v**'s right next to each other. Make sure you don't lift your pencil until you've finished making the letter! Start at the dotted line and slant down, up, down, up. Did you lift your pencil?"

Sound of letter: w as in **walrus**.

ABOUT WALRUSES

"A walrus is the only type of seal with tusks. (Can you remember the other animal we studied with tusks? Yes, it's the elephant.) Tusks are special upper teeth. Walrus tusks grow downward."

"Why does a walrus have tusks? God gave him these special tools to help him when climbing on the ice and to help him defend himself against his enemy the polar bear."

"The walrus spends a lot of time in the water looking for food. It does look like Mr. Walrus could eat a lot of food, doesn't it?"

WALRUS WORK PAGE

"Walruses are dark brown. Their tusks are white, so don't color them. Would you like to draw a rock for Mr. Walrus to sit on?"

PAGES 67 & 68—x

Description of letter: "To make the letter **x**, start at the dotted line and make a slant line down to the solid line. Pick up your pencil and make a slant line the other direction. Did you make both lines from top to bottom?"

Sound of letter: x as in **ibex**. ["No animal's name begins with the **x**, but the **ibex** ends with the **x**."]

ABOUT IBEXES

"The ibex is a mountain goat. It lives in the very high mountains of Europe and Asia. The male ibex has long horns that curve backward. The horns are rough, not smooth like the tusks of elephants and walruses."

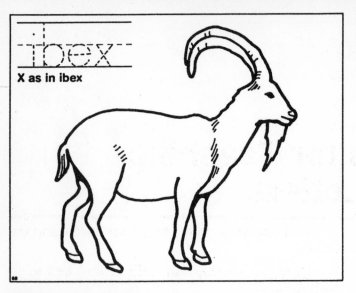

X as in ibex

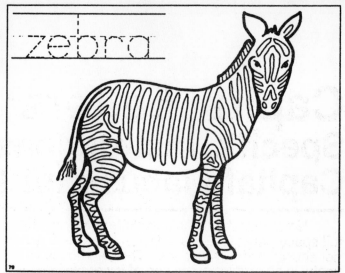

IBEX WORK PAGE

"Color your ibex grey or brown. Behind the ibex draw some tall mountains so it will have a place to live."

PAGES 69 & 70—z

Description of letter: "This is the letter **z**, the last letter of the alphabet! Start at the dotted line. Make a straight line going right, slant down, and then go straight right again. When you can make a **z**, you can write the whole alphabet!"

Sound of letter: z as in **zebra**. ["When you make the sound, your tongue hisses a bit, doesn't it?"]

ABOUT ZEBRAS

"A zebra looks something like a horse, but it is a wild animal that is hard to tame.

"What is the first thing you see that is different about a zebra? Yes, the stripes! For a long time people have been trying to figure out whether a zebra is black with white stripes or white with black stripes. What do you think?

"Why did God give them striped coats? To help them hide easier on the grassy plains of Africa. Their worst enemy is the lion.

"Won't it be nice to get to heaven where all the animals and people can be friends together?"

ZEBRA WORK PAGE

"You'll have to be careful as you color the stripes of this zebra! The dark part should be either black or dark brown. Make sure to leave white stripes on your zebra.

"With dark and white yarn, make a striped mane to glue on your zebra. Maybe you can give him a fluffy yarn bit at the end of his tail, too.

"Finish your page by drawing some grass for the zebra to eat. It should be tall grass if the zebra needs to hide from a lion!"

PAGES 71 & 72—Review

Don't rush through this review lesson! Make sure each child knows how to make each letter correctly and can say the sound(s) of the letter. Watch the students as they make the letters.

PAGES 73 & 74—Alphabet Review

Encourage each student to work slowly and carefully in completing these two alphabet pages. Most children will also profit from taking the time to write the entire alphabet—on a separate sheet of paper—without looking at a sample alphabet. This should be a good sample to save for a parent-teacher conference. Write the date on the paper for later comparison with another sample of the child's handwriting.

PAGES 75 & 76—Review

These pages cover six lowercase letters, chosen from throughout the first part of the book. If your students can remember how to make the letters correctly—and the sound(s) for each—they are probably ready to move into the section on capital letters.

Capital Letters:
Specific Instructions for Teaching Capital Manuscript Letters

Note: because all capital letters occupy the full space between the solid lines, the letters are not shown in the tree house. The tree house is useful in showing the position of lowercase letters because they vary in their size and placement.

INTRODUCTION TO CAPITALS

"We have been all the way through the alphabet once! You can make every lowercase letter.

"Sometimes we need to make larger letters, called *capital letters* or *capitals*. Your name starts with a capital letter. So does the name of our school. You'll soon learn lots of ways to use capitals, so don't you think it's time to learn to make capital letters?

"One thing makes capital letters easy to spot: they are all big. All capitals go from the top solid line clear down to the bottom solid line. No capital letter goes below the bottom solid line. Isn't that an easy thing to remember about capitals?

"Some capital letters are just like their lower-case letters, except larger. But some capitals look quite different from their lowercase letters. That will make it fun to learn each one.

"For the rest of this book we will work with both capital and lowercase letters. In each lesson we will learn a new capital and review the lowercase letter that it goes with. We'll start with a pair that are made the same way."

PAGES 77 & 78—C

Description of letter: "The capital **C** is made exactly like the lowercase **c**, except it fills the space between the solid lines.

Sounds of letter: **C** as in **Cloud**.

C as in **Circle**.

["Would you like to know when there might be a soft **c**? If the c is followed by an e, i, or y, it will sound more like circle than like cat." (Kindergarten children may not remember this rule, but they may remember there is a reason for the different sounds.)]

Here are some words to use for review and ear training.

Hard c: cloud, can, cub, cone, came, carpet, card.

Soft c: circle, citrus, cell, fence, ice, cent, center.

ABOUT CLOUDS

"Do you know how clouds are useful to people? They help the weathermen to know what the weather will be like!

"There are several types of clouds. The ones in this picture are called *cumulus* clouds. They are light and fluffy on top, with a flat base. Cumulus clouds are the ones you usually see when the day is warm and sunny.

"Other clouds show the weatherman that the weather will not be so nice. Watch for cumulus clouds on a day you want to go on a picnic or bike ride!"

CLOUDS WORK PAGE

"First, outline your clouds and color the sky a pretty blue. Then you can make your cumulus clouds thick and fluffy by pasting cotton balls all over them!"

PAGES 79 & 80—G

Description of letter: "The capital **G** is made just like the capital **C**, except the **G** has a line added at the end, forming a table." [Say as you skywrite, "Begin at the 2 o'clock position, go up, around to the line, then to the left halfway into the circle."

Sounds of letter: G as in **Giraffe**.

G as in **goose**.

["The letter usually will be soft when it is followed by an e, i, or y." (Mention this casually for very alert students; don't expect the entire class to grasp the concept.)]

ABOUT GIRAFFES

"What animal do you think of first when I say 'long neck'? The giraffe is a very interesting animal, isn't it?

"The giraffe is the tallest African animal. Can you guess what these tall animals eat? They stretch their long necks and nibble leaves and twigs and sometimes fruit from trees.

"A giraffe has something else that's long (besides its neck). It also has a very long tongue. The big tongue helps it to gather leaves that are high on the tree.

"God gave this animal such a pretty polka-dot coat for a special reason. It's hard to spot a giraffe when it's standing still in the shade of a big tree.

"Giraffes move both legs on one side and then both legs on the other side. It's called *pacing*. At recess see if you can crawl like a giraffe's pacing."

GIRAFFE WORK PAGE

"Color the spots on your giraffe dark brown. The background color should be either tan or yellow. Remember God gave him this coat so he could hide in the shade of trees.

"Draw a tall tree with delicious leaves for your giraffe to nibble. You may want to cut out paper green leaves—or find real green leaves!—and glue them on the page."

PAGES 81 & 82—O

Description of letter: "The capital O is another look-alike with its lowercase letter. It begins at the 2 o'clock position and makes the completed circle."

Sounds of letter: O as in **Owl**.

O as in **orange**.

O as in **do**.

O as in **bone**.

ABOUT OWLS

"Whoooo-whoooo-whoooo knows the bird that makes this sound? Have you ever heard an owl hooting at night?

"Owls have great big eyes that make them look very wise. They can see quite well during the day, but they can see especially well at night. Owls hunt at night. They sit in a tree or on a telephone pole and watch for small animals on the ground. When they see one, they swoop down and kill and eat it. Farmers like owls to live nearby."

OWL WORK PAGE

"Color the owl's feet yellow. The tree branch should be brown.

"To make feathers for your owl, tear tissue or construction paper into small pieces and paste them on your bird. Can you overlap the paper feathers to make it look fluffy?"

PAGES 83 & 84—Q

Description of letter: "The capital **Q** is just like the capital **O**, except it has an added slanting tail at the bottom right of the letter. Make the large circle, then pick up your pencil before adding the tail."

[Since this capital and lowercase letter are so different, it would be well to review the formation of the lowercase **q**.]

Sound of letter: Q as in **Quartz**. "Remember this combination: **qu**."

ABOUT QUARTZ

"You may have seen quartz crystals and thought they were broken glass. Quartz comes in several beautiful colors—purple, yellow, rose, smoky, or clear.

"Quartz is useful. It is used in making glass and sandpaper.

"The next time you're looking for pretty stones, see if you can find some quartz."

QUARTZ WORK PAGE

"What color quartz do you want to make? You can use your purple, yellow, rose, or gray crayon. After you have carefully colored the crystals, add some glue and glitter to make your quartz glisten!"

PAGES 85 & 86—S

Description of letter: "The capital **S** and its lowercase letter are another pair of look-alikes. Begin at the 2 o'clock position and curve around twice without lifting your pencil."

Sound of letter: S as in **Sun**.

ABOUT THE SUN

"Without the heat and light from the sun, there would be no life on Earth! The Earth and the other planets travel around the sun. Traveling around the sun causes Earth's seasons: spring, summer, fall, and winter.

"Your body needs some sunshine every day that the sun shines. It helps to make strong bones. Try to play outside every day that there's sunshine."

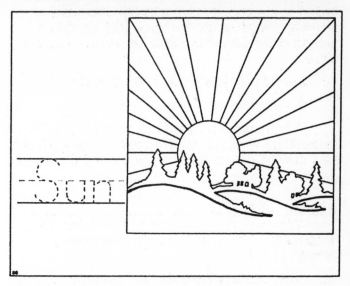

SUN WORK PAGE

"During the day the sun looks bright yellow-orange, but at sunset (or sunrise) it can be many other colors. You can decide how to color this picture. If you want a sunrise (or sunset) picture, you can use pink, orange, purple, and violet crayons to make the sun's rays.

"If you want a special yellow sun, glue pieces of yellow yarn to the lines forming the rays of the sun."

PAGES 87 & 88—A

Description of letter: "The capital **A** looks like an Indian teepee. Start at the attic and make a slanting line clear down to the solid line. Pick up your pencil. Make another slanting line clear down to the solid line. Now make a left-to-right connecting stroke just below the dotted line."

[Since the capital letter is different, it would be good to review the way the lowercase **a** is made.]

Sounds of letter: A as in **Adam**.

A as in **Day**.

ABOUT ADAM

"On the sixth day of Creation Week, the Lord God made man, Adam. The Bible tells us that the Lord God formed man out of the dust of the ground and breathed into him the breath of life (Gen. 2:7).

"God made Adam to enjoy all the animals, fish, birds, and food he had created earlier in the week. Imagine all the good things Adam got to see the first day of his life!"

ADAM WORK PAGE

"Adam was given the job of naming all the animals. After you color Adam, draw your favorite animal next to him. Would that animal be a nice pet for Adam?"

ADDITIONAL ACTIVITY

Give each child a chunk of modeling clay. Ask him to form an Adam figure from the clay. "Didn't God do a good job of molding Adam?"

PAGES 89 & 90—B

Description of letter: "To make a capital **B**, make a straight line down from the solid line. Pick up your pencil. Start at the solid line again and go around and in, around and in." [Sky write this letter as you describe it.]

Sound of letter: B as in **Butterfly**. ["Remember the puff of air you can feel if you hold your hand in front of your mouth when you make the sound?"]

ABOUT BUTTERFLIES

"Have you ever seen the *life cycle* of a butterfly? It's very interesting!

"A butterfly egg hatches into a worm-like *caterpillar*. The caterpillar stuffs itself on leaves for several days. It grows so big it splits its skin! This may happen several times.

"Finally, the caterpillar spins a cozy little nest for itself called a *cocoon*. It curls up inside. You can't see anything happening, but the caterpillar is turning into a butterfly inside that cocoon!

"One day the beautiful butterfly will come out of the cocoon, dry its wings in the sun, and fly away."

Try to find or purchase butterfly eggs so your students can watch the entire life cycle. Make sure that you have appropriate food for the caterpillar. For example, Monarch caterpillars will eat **only** milkweed.

If you come to this lesson in winter, anticipate watching the life cycle of a butterfly in the spring. It's one of the most amazing nature lessons your children can watch, so search around your area to get eggs or caterpillars for your classroom.

BUTTERFLY WORK PAGE

Show colored pictures of several varieties of butterflies from an encyclopedia or butterfly book. Point out common butterflies in your area.

"Color the wings of your butterfly to match each other. Would you also like to draw a picture of a caterpillar and a cocoon below your pretty butterfly?"

PAGES 91 & 92—D

Description of letter: "The capital **D** is different from the lowercase letter. Start with a long straight line from the top solid line to the bottom. Pick up your pencil. Then make a big half circle to finish the letter."

[Review the formation of the lowercase letter.]

Sound of letter: D as in **Dad**.

ABOUT DAD

"Your Dad is a very special person! He may be tall or short. He may have brown, blond, red, or black hair. Maybe he doesn't have much hair at all! But no matter what he looks like, he's your very special Dad!

"What do you especially like about your Dad? Try to think of three things."

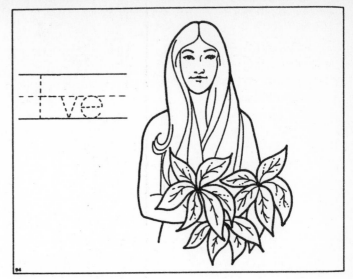

DAD WORK PAGE

"Color the picture of dad to look as much like your Dad as possible. Do you need to add glasses?

"Think of something especially nice you can do for your Dad today." [Be ready with some suggestions: bring in his newspaper; carry in some wood for the fireplace; take him this picture; memorize a Bible verse and say it for him.]

PAGES 93 & 94—E

Description of letter: "The capital **E** is made with four straight lines. The first is down, from the top line to the bottom. Then lift your pencil. Made a straight line at the solid line, from left to right. Pick up your pencil. Make a shorter line across at the dotted line. Pick up your pencil. Make the last line across on the bottom solid line."

[Since this capital letter is different from the lowercase letter, review the formation of the lowercase **e**.]

Sounds of letter: E as in **Eve**.
E as in **Elephant**.

ABOUT EVE

"Do you feel lonely when you are alone? When God first made the world, He knew Adam would be lonely, even with a whole world filled with animals and plants and fish and birds. All these things were wonderful, but they couldn't talk to Adam.

"So God made a companion for Adam. God named the first woman *Eve*. Isn't that a pretty name?

"Adam and Eve lived in a perfect place called the Garden of Eden. They were very happy there."

EVE WORK PAGE

"Eve was a beautiful woman, so color her as carefully as you can. What color hair do you think she had? You may make Eve's hair blond, black, brown, or red.

"Eve is holding a bouquet of leaves. Glue leaves onto your picture. You may make leaves out of construction paper or find real leaves to use."

PAGES 95 & 96—Review

On the review pages for this half of the book, ask the students to match capital and lowercase letters. On the first side of the lesson students draw a line from each capital to its matching lowercase letter. On the back of the page they should write the letter that will complete the pair.

After students have completed the review page, you may wish to give them penmanship paper and have them write the six pairs of capital and lowercase letters without looking in the book.

PAGES 97 & 98—F

Description of letter: "The capital **F** is made almost like the capital **E**, except that it does not have the bottom leg. Start at the top solid line and go straight down to the bottom solid line. Then make a cross line at the top solid line. Make a shorter cross line at the dotted line."

[Since the lowercase **f** is quite different, review its correct formation.]

Sound of letter: F as in **Fish**.

ABOUT FISH

"There are many sizes, shapes, and colors of fish. But they all live in water. Some live in fresh water, in lakes, rivers, and streams. Other kinds of fish live in the salty water of the ocean.

"One funny fish can blow itself up like a balloon! Another one eats its babies!

"All fish breath through *gills*. It's a good thing you have a nose to breathe through since you live on land, isn't it? God gave every creature just what it needs to stay alive!"

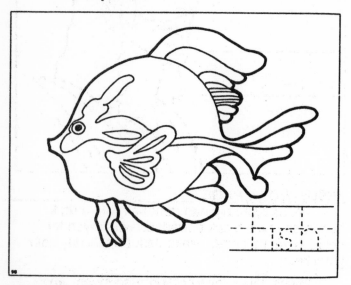

FISH WORK PAGE
"Look in a book about fish or an encyclopedia to see how pretty and colorful fish can be. That will help you decide how to color your fish picture.

"Color your fish as brightly as you can and the water around it blue. Then glue some Cheerios to your page to look like bubbles rising from the mouth of your fish."

ADDITIONAL ACTIVITY
Bring to the classroom a fishbowl or aquarium. Let the children watch the fish. Make sure they can identify the gills.

PAGES 99 & 100—H
Description of letter: "The capital **H** is made with three straight lines. The first two start at the top line and go clear down to the bottom line. Make them a little way apart. Pick up your pencil. Join them with a crosspiece at the dotted line."

[Since this capital is very different from the lowercase letter, review formation of the lowercase **h**.]

Sound of letter: H as in **Heart**.

ABOUT HEARTS
"What makes you the kind of person you are? Maybe it's the one you let control your life. Do you let Jesus help you be a good girl or boy? Does He live in your heart?

"If Jesus is in your heart, it's easier to be kind and loving. It's easier to obey Dad and Mom and your teacher. It's easier to share in the classroom. I want Jesus to live in my heart, don't you?"

HEART WORK PAGE
"Color each heart a different color. Pretend that the biggest heart is yours and paste a sticker of Jesus in that heart. Think of one kind thing you will do today because Jesus is in your heart."

PAGES 101 & 102—I
Description of letter: "The capital **I** is easy to make with three straight lines. First, start at the top solid line and go clear down to the bottom solid line. Lift your pencil. Then make a short cross line at the top line. Pick up your pencil, and make a short cross line at the bottom line."

[Review the lowercase **i** before the students begin writing on their lesson page.]

Sound(s) of letter: I as in **I**, a name I call myself.

I as in **insect**.

ABOUT I

"I is a letter that can be a word all by itself. When you are talking about yourself, you will say, 'I like to help others.' 'I can smile at someone today.'"

Ask the children to tell you some things they can do using this statement, "I can _____." Encourage them to think of themselves as good children who do good things.

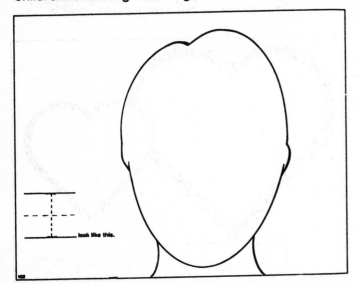

look like this.

I WORK PAGE

"Finish this picture to look like yourself. Is your hair longer? Draw some more! Make sure that you are smiling in your picture. Look in the mirror if you need to see what color eyes and hair you have. Don't leave out your nose and ears!"

PAGES 103 & 104—J

Description of letter: "The capital **J** is just like the lowercase letter, except it's taller and there is no dot. Let's practice sky writing the **J** before we write in our books."

Sound of letter: J as in **Jesus**.

ABOUT JESUS

"What is your favorite story about Jesus? Do you like the one where He fed 5,000 people with the lunch of one little boy? How about the time He healed the daughter of Jairus?

"The Bible tells so many wonderful stories about Jesus and children! Isn't it good to know that Jesus loved children when He was on this earth? Don't you suppose that He **still** loves children? I know He does!"

Jesus

JESUS WORK PAGE

"Jesus probably had dark hair and a dark beard, so use a black or dark brown crayon for coloring your picture. Make Jesus' robe any color you like.

"Since Jesus loved children so much, why don't you draw several children beside Jesus?"

PAGES 105 & 106—K

Description of letter: "The capital **K** is made very much like the lowercase letter. Of course the capital is larger. First, make a long straight line all the way from the top solid line to the bottom solid line. Lift your pencil. Then make a slant line from the top solid line that comes right to the dotted line, then slant it down to the solid line."

Sound of letter: K as in **Koala**.

ABOUT KOALAS

"The koala is a very soft animal that lives in Australia, where the kangaroo also lives. The koala and the kangaroo are alike in another way, too. Both have a pouch where they carry their babies. A baby koala stays in the pouch for several months. When it's older, it rides on its mother's back.

"The koala eats only the leaves and buds from one tree, called a *eucalyptus*. Eucalyptuses grow in California, but not very many other places in the United States."

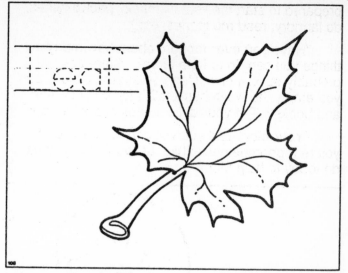

KOALA WORK PAGE

"Color the koala a light brown. Can you draw a baby that looks like its mother riding on her back? Your baby will be smaller, of course.

"Do eucalyptus trees grow where you live? If they do, try to find some leaves to glue onto your picture. If you can find a eucalyptus bud to keep with your picture, it will smell nice!"

PAGES 107 & 108—L

Description of letter: "The capital **L** is a straight line with a leg to rest on! It's quite easy to make. Start at the top line and go straight down to the solid line, then make the leg right on the solid line. Don't pick up your pencil until you've finished the whole letter."

[Review the lowercase letter before students start writing in their book.]

Sound of letter: L as in **Leaf**.

ABOUT LEAVES

"A very important part of a plant is its leaves. Do you know what the job of leaves is?

"God made leaves to be food factories! That's right. A leaf makes food for the plant. The leaf gets energy from the sun. It combines that energy with good things from the soil and water.

"There are three kinds of leaves. Why don't you see if you can find one or more leaves of each kind? We'll look in a book to find the names of different leaves."

1. Broad leaves: oak, maple, etc. These are wide.

2. Narrow leaves: grasses, lilies, onions, etc. These are skinny.

3. Needle leaves: pine needles.

LEAF WORK PAGE

"A maple leaf changes color in the fall, after the first frost. In fall in some parts of the country whole hillsides are gold or red with colored leaves.

"With your water colors, paint this fall leaf. Do you want to mix yellow and red or brown and green?"

PAGES 109 & 110—Review

This matching exercise should be easy if the students have mastered the six capitals just presented. After they have added the correct capital on page 110, you may wish to hand out penmanship paper and have each child write two sets of each of the capital/lowercase pairs just studied.

PAGES 111 & 112—M

This is one of the letters that *A REASON FOR WRITING* recommends making in a non-traditional way. We recommend making the capital **M** with just two strokes, instead of the traditional four. This recommended formation will help students make the transition to the cursive M much easier.

Description of letter: "First, make a long straight line from the top line to the bottom line. Pick up your pencil and start again at the top line. Go slant down, slant up, down."

[Review the formation of the lowercase **m** before starting students on their lesson page. Watch how students are forming their letters.]

Sound of letter: M as in **Mom**.

ABOUT MOM

"How many things can you think of that your Mom does? There are probably quite a few." [Be prepared to start the list: fix meals, pack lunches, do laundry, read me stories, etc.]

"Have you ever thought about how many things you can do to help Mom? There are probably quite a few. Can you set the table? Can you empty the wastebaskets? Pick up your toys and books? Put your dirty clothes in the hamper?

"Your Mom and you will both be happier if you're a good helper. Think of two things you can do today to help Mom."

MOM WORK PAGE

"Think about the color of your Mom's hair before you start coloring your picture. Do you know your Mom's favorite color so you can make the dress that color?

"When you have finished coloring Mom, draw your Mom's favorite flower at the top of the page. Why not give your mother this picture and tell her you love her?"

PAGES 113 & 114—N

Description of letter: "This letter is similar to the capital **M**, except it has one less line. Start at the top line and make a nice straight line clear down to the bottom line. Lift your pencil and start at the top again. Go slant down, up."

[Review the formation of the lowercase letter.]

Sound of letter: N as in **Nuts**.

ABOUT NUTS

Collect as many different nuts in their shell as possible to show the students. [Try for peanuts, walnuts, almonds, pecans, hickory nuts, Brazil nuts.] See how many they can name without help.

At lunchtime, shell and share the different nuts. You may also add cashews and macadamia nuts (if you can afford them!). Talk about how nuts can be eaten [raw, roasted, in nut butters, in baked goods, in candies, and in some main dishes].

If you have access to a peanut butter maker, demonstrate how easy it is to grind roasted peanuts into peanut butter. The children will love getting a sample of fresh peanut butter!

NUT WORK PAGE

"You can look at the nuts on the table to see what colors to make your almond and walnut."

If possible, shell enough walnuts with half shells intact so each child can glue a real walnut shell to his page.

PAGES 115 & 116—P

Description of letter: "This letter is very similar to its lowercase letter. To make a capital **P**, start at the top line and make a straight line clear down to the bottom line. Pick up your pencil. Start at the top and make a half circle that ends at the dotted line."

Sound of letter: P as in **Penguin**. ["This letter is the one that comes out of your mouth in little puffs."]

ABOUT PENGUINS

"The penguin is a very interesting bird. It stands and walks, but it doesn't fly!

"A penguin has webbed feet and flippers to paddle through the water. Penguins live where it is very cold, so they have special feathers to keep them warm.

"Penguins live in groups called *colonies*. Some live right on ice! But God has made them to get along okay even during long winters.

"The father penguin cares for the eggs and the baby chicks. Sometimes a father penguin will move the eggs by carrying them on his feet! Lots of father penguins will huddle together and keep the eggs warm.

"It's fun to watch penguins at the zoo or Sea World because they are such comical birds."

PENGUIN WORK PAGE

"Color your penguin black and white. What color should the bill and feet be?

"Draw two baby penguins following their father to the water. Do you think the babies are going to learn to swim?"

PAGES 117 & 118—R

Description of letter: "The capital **R** is made very much like the capital **P**, except it has an extra leg to lean on! Start with a nice straight line going from the top line to the bottom line. Lift your pencil. Add a half circle, like the **P**, then make a slanted leg to the right."

[Review the formation of the lowercase letter.]

Sound of letter: **R** as in **Rabbit**.

ABOUT RABBITS

"A rabbit is a soft, furry animal. Sometimes a wild rabbit is called a *cottontail* because of its fluffy little tail.

"Although wild rabbits are cute, farmers don't always like them. They love to nibble on the tender little plants in gardens!

"When frightened, a rabbit can jump as far as 10 feet! And if it's being chased, a rabbit may run in a zig-zag manner to get away from its enemy. The rabbit will be safe from dogs or other enemies if it can get to its underground home."

RABBIT WORK PAGE

"Color the inside of your rabbit's ears pink. His fur can be soft brown, gray, white, or spotted.

"Glue a cotton ball on your rabbit's tail to make it look like a real cottontail!"

PAGES 119 & 120—T

Description of letter: "This letter is very much like its lowercase letter. The capital **T** is easy to make! Just make a nice straight line from the top line to the bottom. Life your pencil. Make a cross line right at the top line."

Sound of letter: **T** as in **Tree**.

ABOUT TREES

"Trees are the largest plants. They're good for many things. Can you think of three?" [shade, lumber, fruit, nuts, etc.]

"There are many different kinds of trees. You can tell many trees by their shapes. Do you know the names of trees around your school and home? A book from the library will help.

"Each state has a state tree. Find out the official state tree for your state."

TREE WORK PAGE

"Color the shade tree. Add a nice lawn under the tree and several kinds of birds in the sky. Do you think it might be a good place for a kite to be flying? Design a pretty kite you'd like to fly."

PAGES 121 & 122—U

Description of letter: "This capital letter is just like its lowercase letter, only taller. That makes it easy, doesn't it? Start at the top line and come down, around and up, and back down again. Don't lift your pencil until you've made the whole letter!"

Sound of letter: "Sometimes the sound of this letter is controlled by the letter **r**. Listen to the sound of our word today: **Sea Urchin**. Do you hear the **r** sound?"

ABOUT SEA URCHINS

"This is an animal that looks like a flower and lives in the sea! Have you ever seen a sea urchin? God made some very interesting creatures to live in the oceans!

"A sea urchin is shaped like a ball with long wavy spines growing all over it. The spines wiggle in the water as the waves come and go. It's fun to watch!"

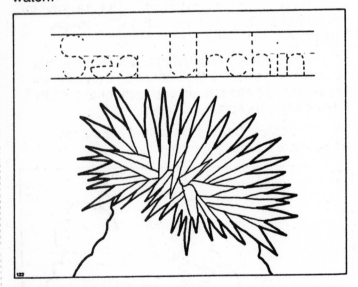

SEA URCHIN WORK PAGE

"Sea urchins may be lavender, pink, or pale blue. Choose the color you want yours to be. Then color in seawater around the sea urchin and add some seaweed and fish."

PAGES 123 & 124—Review

Go over the directions for the review pages before the students open their books. By now they should be familiar with the exercises.

PAGES 125 & 126—Y

This is another capital letter where we recommend a non-traditional method of formation. It is made with only two strokes instead of the traditional three.

Description of letter: "This capital letter is a little different from its lowercase letter. Start at the top line and make a **v** with the point at the dotted line. Pick up your pencil. Add a tail straight down from the point of the **v**."

Sound of letter: Y as in **Yucca**.

ABOUT YUCCA

"The yucca is a plant that grows in the desert, where there is lots of sand and not much water. However, the yucca plant stays green all year.

"When the yucca blooms, it has whitish bell-shaped flowers. The blossoms open at night. They smell good."

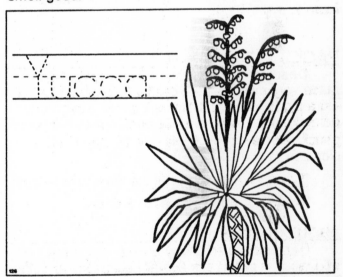

YUCCA WORK PAGE

"Color the leaves on your yucca green and the trunk brown. Would you like to make your page into a desert scene? Spread a little glue on your page and immediately sprinkle it with clean sand. Glue some bits of popped popcorn to make the blossoms. Your yucca is now blooming in a desert!"

PAGES 127 & 128—V

Description of letter: "This is another look-alike pair of letters. Just make the capital larger than the lowercase **v**. Let's review how it's made: Start at the top line and slant down, slant up without lifting your pencil."

Sound of letter: V as in **Volcano**.

ABOUT VOLCANOES

"A volcano is usually a cone-shaped mountain. When the volcano explodes, or *erupts*, melted rocks and fire are thrown many hundreds of feet into the air. Ashes fill the air for hundreds of miles. Then the melted rock, called *lava*, flows down the side of the mountain.

"Scientists don't know all about volcanoes, but they do know there is a lot of power in a volcano. You don't want to be close when a volcano erupts!"

[If there is a volcanic mountain in your area, describe it to the class. Tell them that it's been inactive for many, many years, so they don't have to worry about its erupting.]

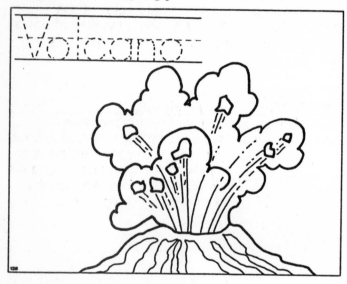

VOLCANO WORK PAGE

"Color the mountain brown and the fire exploding red and yellow. The streams of lava flowing over the mountain should be red-orange.

"To finish your picture, you may want to glue small rocks and toothpicks on the eruption."

PAGES 129 & 130—W

Description of letter: "This is another pair of capital and lowercase letters that are made the same. Of course, the capital is larger.

"Start at the top line and make your letter with a slant down, slant up, slant down, slant up stroke.

Don't lift your pencil until you've made the whole letter!"

Sound of letter: W as in **Watermelon**.

ABOUT WATERMELONS

"Have you ever seen a watermelon growing on its vine in the field? The vine can be large and have several melons on it.

"Some watermelons are solid green on the outside, and some are striped green and white. But on the inside a good watermelon is bright red!"

If it's the right season, serve the children slices of watermelon at lunchtime. Have them save the seeds and count them. Who got the most seeds; who got the fewest? Did any two children get the same?

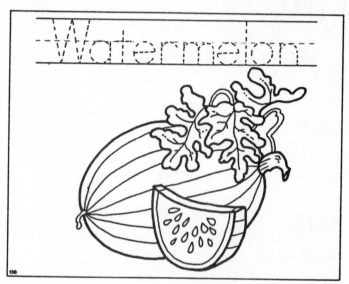

WATERMELON WORK PAGE

"It looks like you get to color a striped water-melon today. Use your darkest green crayon for the outside of the melon.

"If you can get watermelon seeds, glue them to your nice red slice of melon."

PAGES 131 & 132—X

Description of letter: "The capital letter is just like the lowercase letter, except it's larger. It's two slanting lines that go from the top line to the bottom line. Pick up your pencil after the first slanted line. Then make another one."

Sound of letter: "No animal name starts with this sound, but **Fox** ends with the **x** sound."

ABOUT FOXES

"Do you know that a fox is a type of dog? Foxes have bushy tails and large pointed ears and long noses.

"Some foxes are reddish brown and others are gray. Because their fur is so soft and long, hunters trap foxes to sell the fur.

"Did you know that Jesus talked about foxes? In Matthew He says that foxes have their homes, but that He didn't have a place to lay His head."

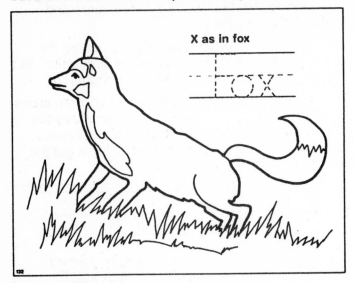

X as in fox

FOX WORK PAGE

"Would you like to make a red fox or a gray fox? Either is okay. This fox seems to be watching something. Draw what you think it might be."

PAGES 133 & 134—Z

Description of letter: "Another look-alike pair of capital and lowercase letters! Make the capital **Z** just like the lowercase one, but make it fill from the top line to the bottom.

"It's fun to zig-zag the **Z**! Start at the top line and make a nice straight line along the top, then make a long slant line and turn back along the bottom line. Don't lift your pencil!"

Sound of letter: Z as in **Zinnia**.

ABOUT ZINNIAS

"Zinnias are bright, colorful flowers. They're easy to grow, too. We'll grow some on the windowsill of our classroom!"

This is an easy gardening project. At some times of the year you can get bedding packs of zinnias at a garden center. Or, if you have time before the school year ends, start seeds in foam cups or tin cans. That way each child can have his very own zinnia to care for.

This is a good time to talk about other flowers, too. If you have space and inclination, why not plant a small flower garden near your classroom?

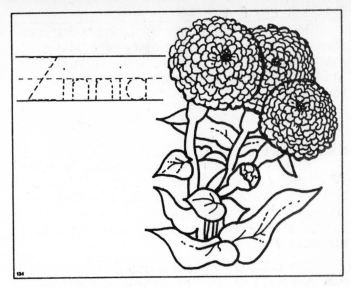

ZINNIA WORK PAGE

"Color the leaves and stems of your zinnias green. See the bud that's almost ready to open? Color it a bright color.

"Instead of coloring your three zinnias, why not make bright petals from colored construction paper? Tear it into tiny bits about the size of zinnia petals. Glue each one to the flower. What a pretty garden you've made!"

PAGES 135 & 136—Review

When students have finished the review pages, give them penmanship paper and ask them to write the whole alphabet with capital letters and lowercase letters side by side. Circulate around the room as the children are writing to make sure that each one has correct formation of the letters.

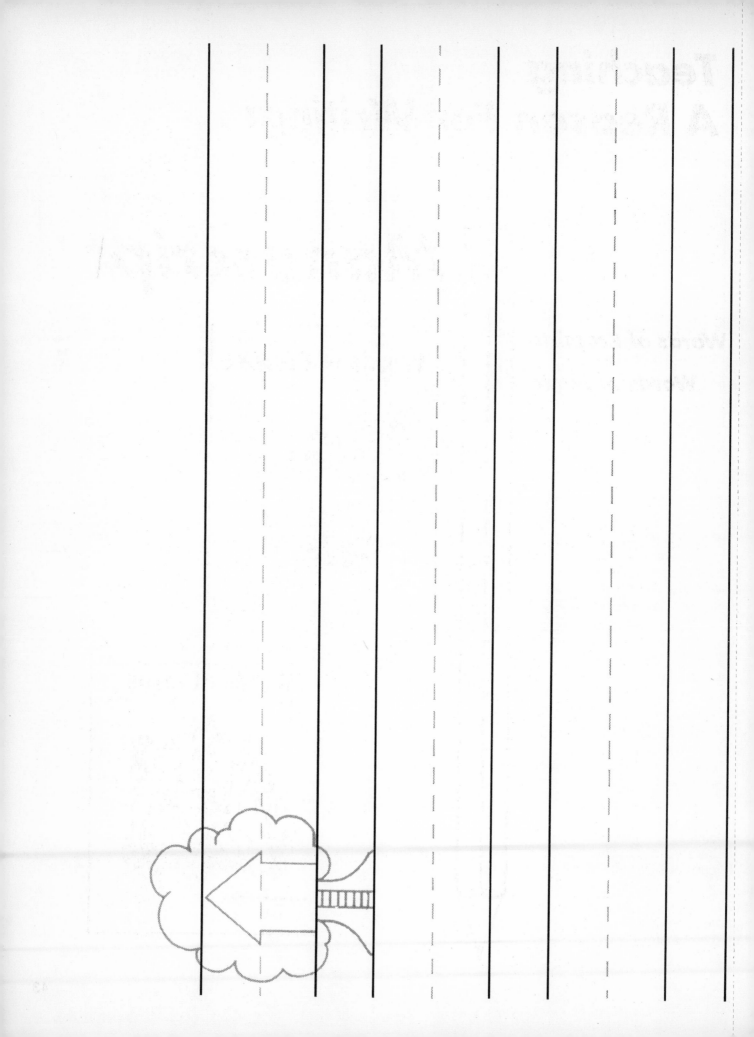

Teaching
A Reason For Writing:

Manuscript

Words of Promise

Words of Jesus

ADVENTURES IN HANDWRITING FROM PSALMS & PROVERBS
Words of Promise
LESSON, PRACTICE & BORDER BOOK   MANUSCRIPT

BY CAROL ANN RETZER & EVA HOSHINO

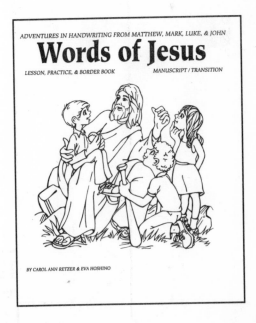

ADVENTURES IN HANDWRITING FROM MATTHEW, MARK, LUKE, & JOHN
Words of Jesus
LESSON, PRACTICE, & BORDER BOOK   MANUSCRIPT / TRANSITION

BY CAROL ANN RETZER & EVA HOSHINO

Introducing the Student Workbooks

The manuscript *Student Workbooks* are divided into three sections: practice pages weekly lessons, and border sheets.

Begin with the practice pages in the first section of the book. It should take eight weeks to complete this section, using a page a day four days a week. The fifth handwriting period should be used for review. (If practice pages are used five days a week, the practice section can be completed in six weeks.)

These two books may be used on an alternating basis in a multi-grade classroom. However, because of the special readiness needs of some second graders, *Words of Jesus* also includes introductory cursive lessons. There are enough lessons for a complete year of manuscript, and a full semester of cursive, so you may introduce cirsove at any time during second semester.

If cursive is being introduced in second grade, see page 77, "Preparing Students for Transition to Cursive Writing".

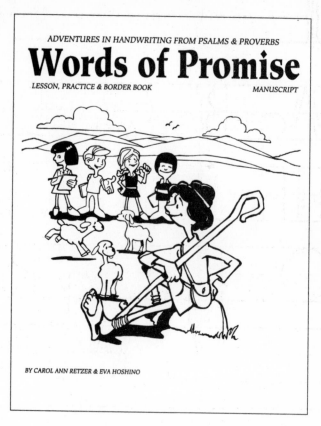

ADVENTURES IN HANDWRITING FROM PSALMS & PROVERBS

Words of Promise

LESSON, PRACTICE & BORDER BOOK   MANUSCRIPT

BY CAROL ANN RETZER & EVA HOSHINO

Teaching Cursive Optional

The use of these cursive pages is optional. *Words of Jesus* contains a complete year of manuscript lessons as well as the cursive transition lessons. The transition section is perforated and may be removed if the teacher does not choose to use them.

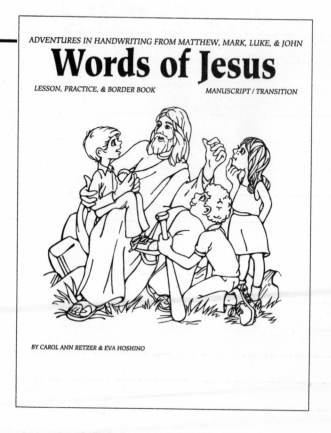

ADVENTURES IN HANDWRITING FROM MATTHEW, MARK, LUKE, & JOHN

Words of Jesus

LESSON, PRACTICE, & BORDER BOOK   MANUSCRIPT / TRANSITION

BY CAROL ANN RETZER & EVA HOSHINO

Manuscript Letter Formation

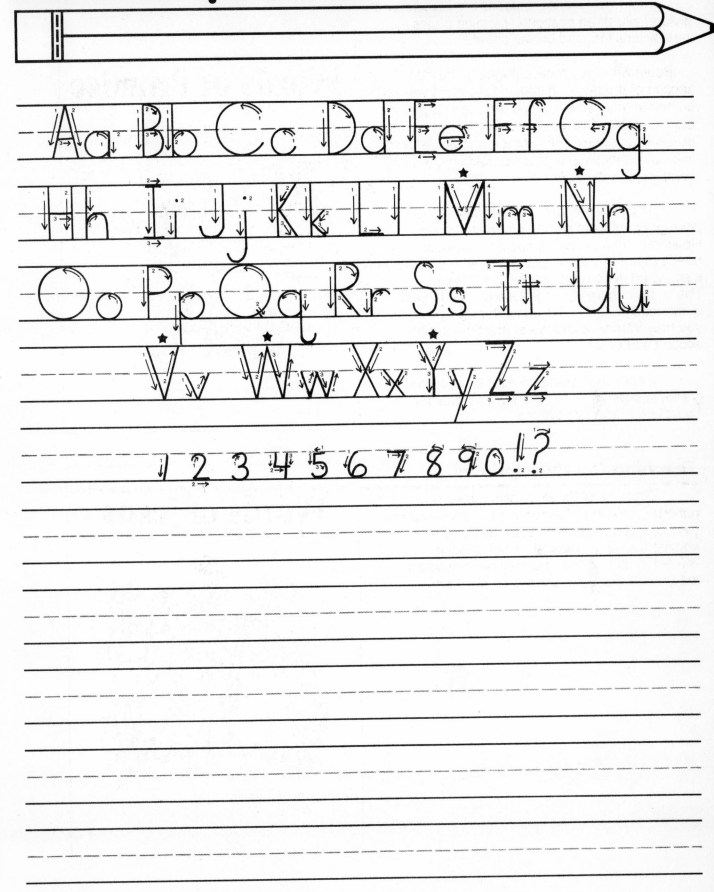

Improving Pre-Writing Readiness

Before learning to write, children need to participate in small- and large-motor assignments that don't require paper and pencil. Here are some appropriate hand-eye coordination activities that will enhance pre-writing skills.

- Working puzzles
- Building with blocks
- Cutting with scissors
- Pasting pictures and shapes
- Stringing beads
- Painting (with finger paints or watercolors)
- Lacing and tying shoes
- Bouncing and catching a ball
- Drawing on the chalkboard or easel
- Recognizing and naming letters of the alphabet
- Copying simple stick-circle drawings (see samples below) that teach the direction of the stroke. This is important groundwork for manuscript writing.

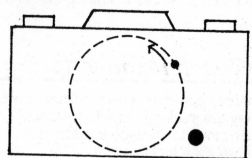

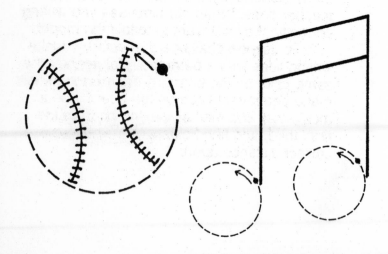

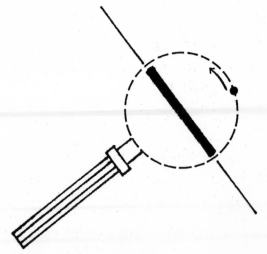

Readiness

You can help students form a solid foundation for handwriting even before they can read. While talking to the class, write down the key word or sentence. This will help the students store up correct direction and sequence of strokes and provide the visual imagery of finished letters and words. As this is done, students begin unconsciously to comprehend correct form, proper arrangement, and even punctuation.

Students can enjoy visual readiness activities that focus on the alphabet—seeing the letter, naming the letter, and rhyming with the letter—without writing it. Experience at the chalkboard or easel will help children to develop necessary pre-writing skills without wearing them out with needless paperwork.

When students are ready for pencil-and-paper activities, give them large unlined sheets and either felt markers or crayons. They can then progress to lined paper and pencil.

Why Teach Manuscript?

Children can most easily imitate in writing what they are seeing in reading. Manuscript forms are close to the type in beginning readers, so it's a logical starting point for writing.

Common obstacles in learning to read may be eliminated through a multisensory approach to learning manuscript handwriting. Many of the exercises used in *A REASON FOR WRITING* will also strengthen students' reading skills.

Use an Alphabet Chart

From the beginning of the school year, display an alphabet chart at the front of the classroom. This is particularly helpful for students with reversal problems.

Make Name Cards

A person's name is probably the most important thing he or she ever writes. When students write their names, encourage them to use a capital letter to begin, then write the rest in lowercase letters.

To help students write their names correctly, tape a model of each student's name to his or her desk, where it can be seen many times a day. This name card can also serve as a locater. You can say, for example, "Begin writing on the left side of your paper — your name tag is on the left of your desk."

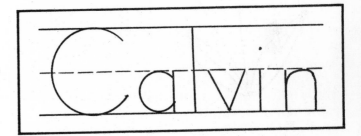

Write to Be Imitated

The teacher should be careful always to write clearly—whether at the chalkboard or on paper—and to avoid extra curls on letters. Many students try to imitate whatever the teacher does. When students see you writing correctly, they will want to follow the model.

To use the chalkboard effectively, make writing lines with a permanent felt marker the same color as the board. If it's impractical to make permanent lines on the board, use a music-staff line marker, putting chalk in the first, third, and fifth holders to make lines the correct distance apart.

Exception to Traditional Forms

Manuscript writing is the closest system to that used in books the student is learning to read. If the next step in written communication (after manuscript) is cursive writing, transition should be made as easy as possible. When logical strokes in manuscript have been mastered and visual readiness activities have been provided, the transition to cursive should be smooth.

Forming letters correctly allows easier transition from manuscript to cursive writing. You will discover that *A REASON FOR WRITING* suggests non-traditional formations for five capital letters — **M, N, V, W,** and **Y.** These non-traditional formations are starred on the chart on page 10.

Consider for a moment the capital **M.** If only down strokes are used, (as in the traditional formation) the child's motor skills have to be refined for him to find — and meet — a mid-point.

In *A REASON FOR WRITING* we are suggesting the strokes for **M** be down, down-up-down, as shown below.* The pencil is lifted only once, rather than three times. Take a moment and try the traditional method for making this letter; then try the way recommended by *A REASON FOR WRITING.* Now compare this new method with the natural cursive formation. See how the recommended manuscript formation can provide an easy transition to cursive?

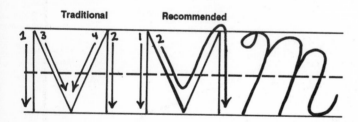

The **V** should go down-up, just as you would see recommended on a cursive-writing chart, rather than the traditional form of down, down, meeting at the point.

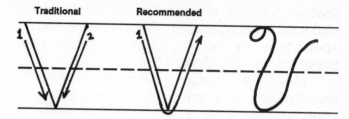

The recommended **W** goes down-up-down-up without lifting the pencil. Again, this is similar to cursive formation. The traditional formation is down, down, down, down.

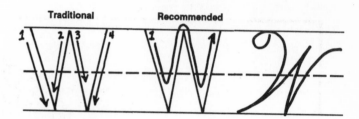

The recommended **N** is down, down-up rather than down, down, down.

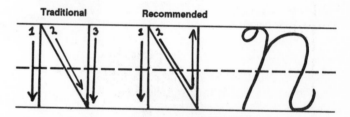

The recommended **Y** is down-up, down. The traditional is down, down, down.

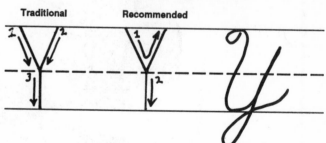

It is important to have school-wide consistency in teaching handwriting. If, after studying the non-traditional forms suggested here, you wish to adopt this method, meet with other teachers who will also be teaching manuscript writing. Decide as a group which forms to teach, and stick with that decision. It is important that students not be taught alternate ways to make the same letters!

*In describing handwriting strokes, a comma indicates that the pencil is lifted; a hyphen indicates a continuing stroke.

The First Week of Handwriting

Since most of the strokes in manuscript are lines and circles, encouraging students to practice these to learn proper direction will make handwriting easier. Don't be afraid to spend time the first week having the students make circles and straight lines.

Make the introduction to writing as non-stressful as possible. Begin by blowing soap bubbles. Draw attention to their shape and beauty. Spend time letting students describe the bubbles—round, shiny, colorful, etc. Describing the bubbles will encourage them to think about and remember the shape.

Next, skywrite some bubbles. Put the pointer finger of your writing hand a little higher than eye level and make the shape. Demonstrate this to students and have them also skywrite bubbles. You may face the class and make the circle in the opposite direction. Or you may stand with your back slightly turned and skywrite, watching the class over your shoulder.

Make the circles—or bubbles—starting at the 2 o'clock position and moving in a counterclockwise direction. As students practice, you can observe whether or not they understand position and direction.

Continue this process until the class thoroughly knows direction. You can say: "Start at the 2 o'clock position, go up to the left, and around." Encourage students to repeat the verbal description of the strokes.

Next students can draw bubbles, using unlined paper and crayons or felt markers. Instruct students to make as many different-colored bubbles as they can, and in several sizes. They might think of them as many sizes and colors of balloons.

Again, stress beginning at the 2 o'clock position (show students a clock-face), going up, and around. Monitor the class to see who may be having trouble. You may need to put your hand over the student's hand to help him or her develop the correct movement. This activity will reinforce the positioning and direction of circles.

When students have perfected bubbles, start them on sticks—straight lines. Sticks should begin at the top and go down. Skywrite this motion before students begin writing on paper. Verbalize the stroke: "Begin at the top and go straight down." Students should first make a lot of sticks on unlined paper.

After students have practiced both bubbles and sticks on unlined paper, they are ready to practice on lined paper. They should make a page of bubbles, then a page of sticks, and finally a page of alternating bubbles and sticks.

An extended activity that combines both bubbles and sticks will reinforce what has just been learned: Ask students to draw pictures using only sticks and bubbles. They may use straight lines going directions other than down. *(See sample drawings on this page.)*

Don't eliminate these simple-sounding exercises! Time spent early with these exercises will pay off later in good letter formation.

Proper spacing is another important aspect of writing. As students begin writing bubbles and sticks, they need to be aware of correct spacing.

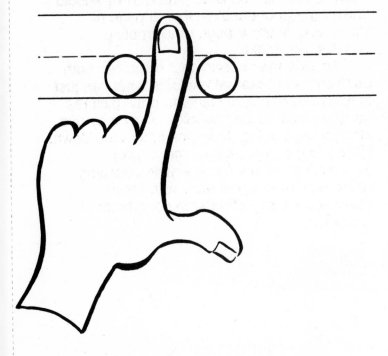

Here's an easy way for students to gauge their own spacing. Make sure each child knows which finger is the **index finger** (the one next to the thumb). Suggest that each student use the index finger **of the hand that doesn't hold the pencil** to measure spacing. Have the student write the first figure, then put his or her index finger next to it. The next figure begins immediately to the right of his or her index finger. Eventually, the student's eye will automatically help with spacing and this separate step will no longer be necessary.

Writing Sample

At the beginning of the year or semester, have the student write as much of the alphabet as possible—both capital and lowercase letters. This is a pre-test. Also, ask the student to write his or her own name on the paper.

Save this sample of writing (with the date on it) for the first parent-teacher conference, usually at the end of the first nine weeks. Then, just before the conference, have the student write his or her name and the alphabet again. Date this sheet also. Show these two samples to the parents.

This exercise will also help you to keep in mind the student's starting point. Each student should be evaluated **on his or her own progress**—as compared with earlier work—rather than compared against the model.

Please see page 74 for Manuscript Black Line Masters to use with students needing extra practice or for **pre-** and **post-testing.**

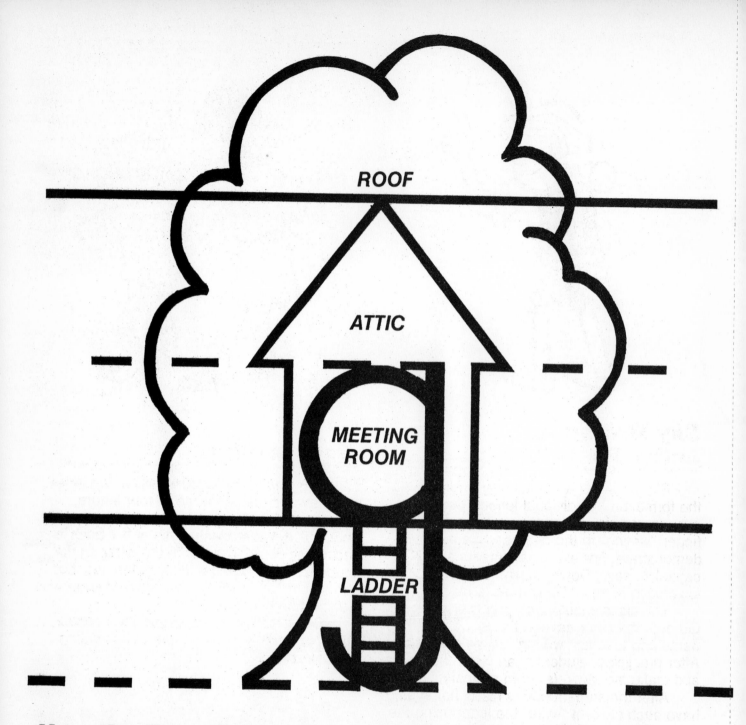

ROOF

ATTIC

MEETING ROOM

LADDER

How the Tree House Can Help in Letter Positioning

The concept of the tree house is helpful in explaining to beginning writers the position of lowercase letters in relation to the lines. The tree house is used throughout the manuscript *Student Workbooks.*

Explain that the main part of the letter is written within the confines of the tree house. Some letters begin at the top of the roof; others begin in the meeting room; and still others begin in the meeting room and go down the ladder to the ground.

Students will grasp the concept of the new letter quickly if you say, "The **b** begins at the roof and goes to the bottom of the meeting room" or "Shouldn't your **g** go clear down to the ground?"

You may wish to draw a tree house on an overhead transparency or the chalkboard and demonstrate each new letter as it is introduced.

Please see page 41 for a Tree House Black Line Master for use with students needing extra practice.

Sky Writing for Letter Formation

Sky writing is a helpful way of practicing the formation of individual letters. Demonstrate the letter formation with your pointer finger "writing" in the air. Describe as you demonstrate. For example, when making the capital **A**, say, "Down, down, across." For the lowercase **b**, say, "Down-up-around."

The class should then practice together. Go over the letter several times, with the students and teacher "writing" at the same time. After practicing, students can close their eyes and make the stroke(s) from memory.

After the student opens his or her eyes, have each student "write" the letter using the pointer finger to "write" on the palm of the hand that he or she **doesn't** use for holding the pencil. This should be practiced several times, with the student repeating the description of the stroke(s).

Back Writing

This is a game students will enjoy. After you have introduced three or four letters, choose one student to come to the front of the room. Turn the student so his or her back is facing the class. Then write the letter on the student's back with big, definite strokes. Let the student try to tell the class which letter was outlined on his back.

Once students understand the concept, they can work in pairs, taking turns "writing" and guessing.

Practice Pages

This section emphasizes formation of all letters and numbers. For first graders, it is their introduction to writing letters; for second graders, it is a necessary and good review of the alphabet and numbers.

Beginning dots are printed on the practice pages to help students start the letter at the correct position in the line and with the correct spacing. On the first few practice pages, expect that students may have letters touching. Encourage neatness, however, and remind them to stay within the lines. **Students will usually live up to the teacher's expectations, so your expectations should be clearly stated.**

When grading, circle the best letters, not the worst. Emphasizing the positive rather than the negative is helpful. Write on a student's paper: "These are your best letters. Keep up the good work!" Even though a beginner may not be able to read the comment, he/she will enjoy having it read to him/her and will be encouraged.

It's important for students to do this section! You'll be fighting faulty letter formation all year unless you emphasize it the first two months of school. In a multi-grade or combination-grade classroom, it is beneficial for the class to be kept together throughout the practice pages.

In a later section of this book, detailed letter formation directions are given for each letter. Because many children are auditory learners, you should repeat the stroke formation aloud. Then instruct the class to move with the letter, using sky writing (See page 53) or the chalkboard to create a mental picture.

Many circle letters can be described easily with the aid of a clock face. If a large clock is not clearly visible, draw a model and place it in plain sight.

The tree house is also helpful for positioning new lowercase letters.

If you notice a child having difficulty with the direction of strokes of a particular letter, give him or her special attention. Some students may need only additional practice on paper. Please see page 74 for a Manuscript-spaced Black Line Master for students who are

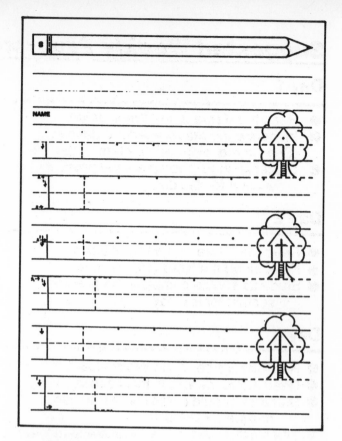

needing extra practice.) Others may need to go through these steps again with you:

- Say the letter.

- Describe the stroke(s) used in making the letter.

- Let the student move with the letter in one or more of these ways:
  - Encourage him/her to write the letter withhis/her pointer finger in the palm of his/her hand.
  - Let him/her write the letter in a box of sand or salt.
  - Ask him/her to finger-paint the letter several times.
  - Let him/her trace clay or plastic letters.

Note: The practice pages of *Words of Promise* (page 25) and *Words of Jesus* (page 33) contain one sheet that is blank on one side so the student can write the lesson, decorate it with a colorful design, fold it like a letter, and fasten it shut with a sticker. The student can then proudly share the message with someone special.

Suggested Weekly Program Using the Lesson Section

Day 1

- Read the Verse of the Week aloud.
- Introduce the practice letter or letters. (See "Introducing New Letters," page 58.)
- Students should complete the practice section for the day.

Day 2

- Read the Verse of the Week aloud.
- Read aloud the words for practice.
- Students should complete the practice section for the day.

Day 3

- Read the Verse of the Week aloud.
- Read aloud the words for practice.
- Students should complete the practice section for the day.
- The teacher should be available to monitor individual students for correct letter formation.

Day 4

- Read the Verse of the Week aloud.
- Students should write the verse on practice paper once or twice.
- Let the students choose a Scripture border sheet from the back of the book. Encourage them to do their best writing of the week on the Scripture border sheet.

Day 5

- Read the Verse of the Week aloud.
- Encourage the students to decorate their Scripture border sheets.
- Discuss what the students can do with their completed verses. (See "Ways to Share," page 73.)

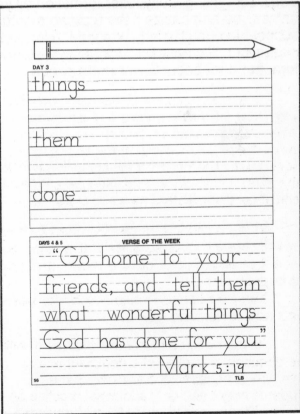

55

Using the Lesson Section

When students have mastered the alphabet on the practice pages, they are ready to move on to the lesson section.

First graders should complete the practice pages before starting on the lesson section.

You may choose to start second graders with the lesson section and use the practice pages for backup practice.

In a multi-grade classroom, both grades may be practicing together. Second graders will benefit from the review of letter formations. In this instance, you may wish to utilize the extended activities incorporated with the detailed outline of letter formation as well as in the section below.

The lessons in the *Student Workbooks* outline the work for each day, so a minimum of teacher direction is needed once the letter direction is reviewed and stressed.

Notice that review lessons are starred. You may wish to skip any or all of the review lessons.

Extended Activities

One or more of these extended activities may be used in connection with each weekly lesson and may be assigned to all or part of the class:

- *Write a sentence using the practice words for today.*

- *Use a dictionary to help you find three more words beginning with the letter or letters used today.*

- *Put the practice words for the day [or week] in alphabetical order.*

Introducing New Letters

As you present the letter of the day, be sure to stress the letter's name and sound. The order of strokes to make the letter should be emphasized. Make sure each student understands where the letter is positioned on the line. (The tree house will help in explaining this concept.)

Here's a suggested sequence of instruction:

- The teacher writes the letter and says its name.

- The teacher describes the stroke(s).

- The teacher skywrites the letter. (See page 53.)

- The teacher and students skywrite together, with the teacher watching the students to see who might be having trouble.

- The students practice the letter on paper.

Encourage Carry-Over To Other Work

Encourage students to write neatly on all their work. Remind them that writing neatly only in handwriting class is similar to being good only one day of the week.

If evaluation is made simple enough, students can look at their own work and evaluate it on their own. Here are three simple check-yourself questions every child can learn:

- Is the writing neat?

- Are the letters and words spaced correctly?

- Is each letter straight?

Improving Student Self-Image

When the students can be proud of their work, they will feel good about themselves. Your positive evaluation and help will add to a healthy self-image. The weekly Scripture border sheets — with a peel-off note of encouragement — will show both the students and their parents how much their handwriting is improving.

Description of Manuscript Forms

- Manuscript letters are composed of straight lines, circles, and parts of circles.

- Capitals and tall letters are twice the size of small letters (with the exception of the letter **t**).

- The beginning vertical and slanting lines are made from the top downward.

- As much of a letter as possible should be made with a single stroke, without picking up the pencil point. The lowercase exceptions are **f**, **i**, **j**, **k**, **t**, and **y**. Using longer, smoother strokes in manuscript makes the transition to cursive writing easier.

- Letters in a word should not touch each other.

- Words should be spaced for easy reading.

Order of Letter Introduction

The first pages in the practice section review circles and lines. Then letters are introduced in this logical order, based on the way they are formed: **o**, **a**, **d**, **g**, **q**, **c**, **e**, **b**, **p**, **i**, **t**, **l**, **h**, **r**, **n**, **m**, **f**, **u**, **j**, **y**, **v**, **w**, **k**, **s**, **x**, and **z**.

Extra Practice

When a student is having diffculty with one particular letter or stroke, refer him to similar letter formations. The charts on pages 59 and 60 show these "letter families" you may assign for additional practice.

Sentence Evaluation

The sentence on the pencil contains all the letters of the alphabet. It is good to use for an overall evalution of handwriting. Ask students to write the sentence at the beginning of the grading period and again at the end. Any specific letter problems students have should show up in this sentence evaluation.

Grading

For evaluation, keep a folder of samples for each student, with pages from the beginning and ending of each grading period. When it's time to give grades, you can evaluate each student **on his or her own progress**. If the student is regularly taking home Scripture border sheets, parents should be aware of their child's handwriting improvement.

Some teachers have found the 10-point grading scale (below) helpful. It covers all 5 areas for evaluation and allows students to know exactly how they will be evaluated. (Please see page 74 for a Black-Line Master for duplication and use in your classroom.)

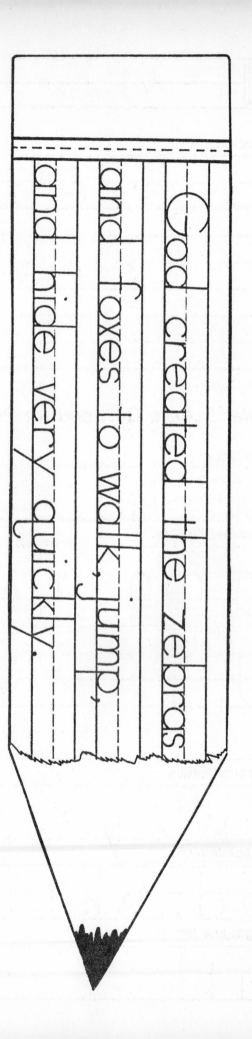

God created the zebras, and foxes to walk, jump, and hide very quickly.

Handwriting Evaluation Form

2 points possible for each:

Alignment
Letter stays on the line.   _____

Slant
Letters have the same slant.   _____

Size
Capital and lowercase letters
are the right size.   _____

Shape
Letters are shaped correctly
and neatly.   _____

Spacing
Letters and words are spaced
and spelled correctly.   _____

TOTAL _____

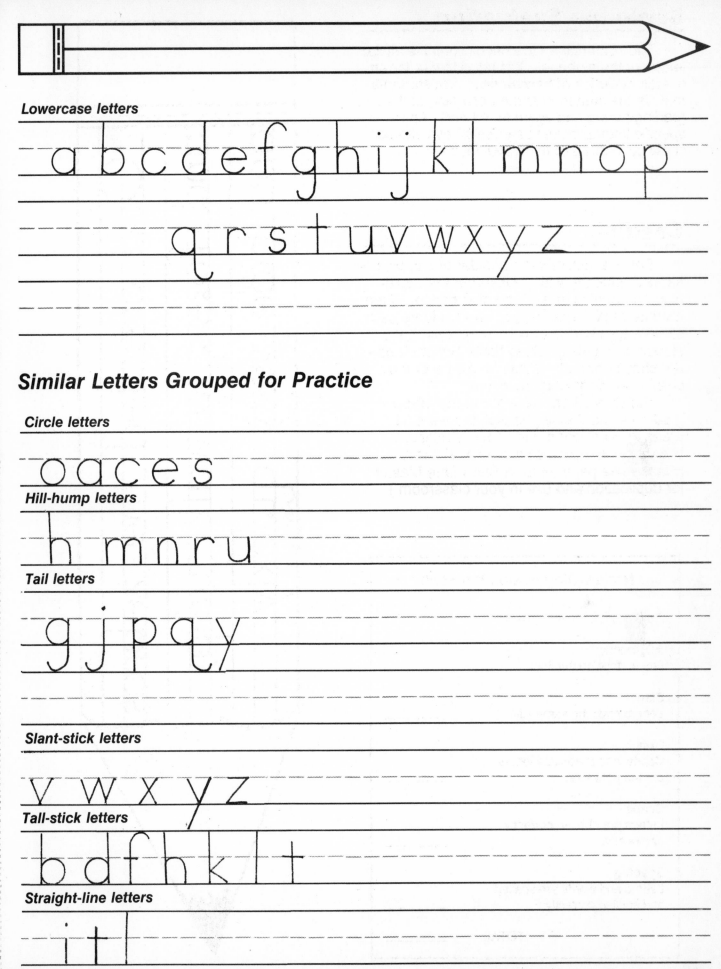

Lowercase letters

a b c d e f g h i j k l m n o p

q r s t u v w x y z

Similar Letters Grouped for Practice

Circle letters

o a c e s

Hill-hump letters

h m n r u

Tail letters

g j p q y

Slant-stick letters

v w x y z

Tall-stick letters

b d f h k l t

Straight-line letters

i t

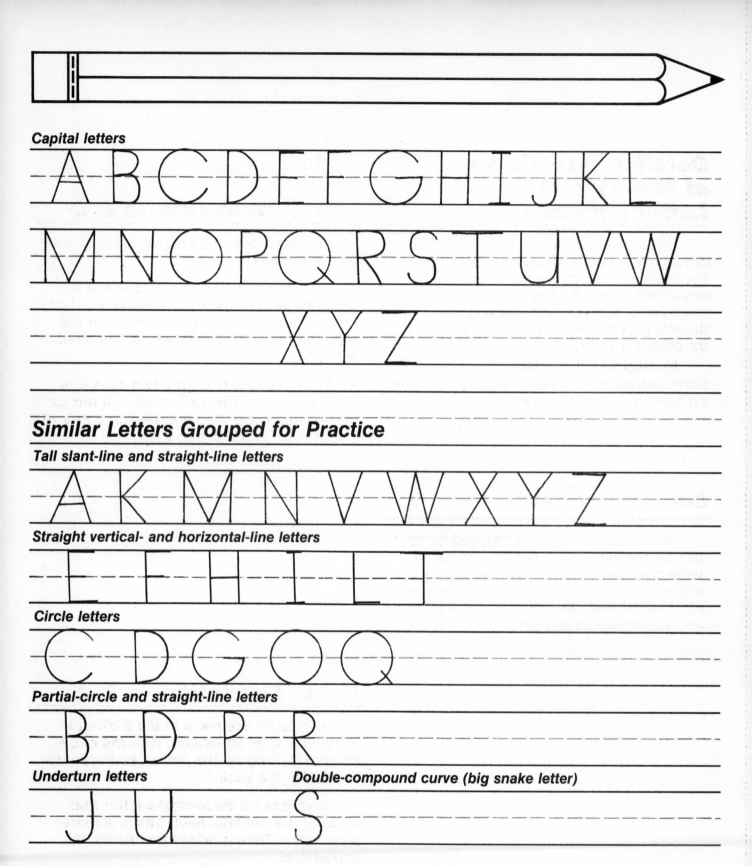

Capital letters

A B C D E F G H I J K L M N O P Q R S T U V W X Y Z

Similar Letters Grouped for Practice

Tall slant-line and straight-line letters

A K M N V W X Y Z

Straight vertical- and horizontal-line letters

E F H I L T

Circle letters

C D G O Q

Partial-circle and straight-line letters

B D P R

Underturn letters

J U

Double-compound curve (big snake letter)

S

Detailed Description of Manuscript Letter Formation

This section will prepare you to introduce formation for each lowercase and capital letter. The letters are discribed in the order in which they appear in the *Student Workbooks.* Specific directions for the teacher to repeat to the students are enclosed in quotation marks and printed in **bold italic.**

In describing the strokes, a comma indicates that the pencil should be lifted; a hyphen indicates a continuing stroke.

Extended Activities

Extended activities are included for your use as needed. The extended activities involve small-motor skills which will enhance writing skills. Each is marked with this symbol: ✍ . You will need to distribute paper and any additional supplies needed.

Letter Formation—o & O

o—*"Start at the 2 o'clock position and go up-around."*

O—*"The capital O is made in exactly the same way as the lowercase letter. Just make it larger—clear up to the top of the roof and down to the bottom of the meeting room."*

✍ *"Draw your eyes. Do the two eyes look like o's? You may need to look in a mirror to see what color they are. Design a pair of glasses you might like to wear."*

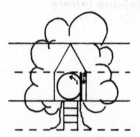

Letter Formation—a & A

a—*"Begin like the o at the 2 o'clock position and go up-around with the circle. Without picking up the pencil, continue up-down with the stick."*

A—*"Here's a three-stroke letter that starts at the top line. Slant down. Another slant down. Then a bridge just below the dotted line."*

✍ *"A stands for the ark and animals that were in it. Read the story in your favorite Bible story book and then draw an ark and some animals. There should be seven of some animals and two of others. Will you have room for all of them in your picture?"*

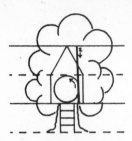

Letter Formation—d & D

d—"This letter is almost like the a, except the stick goes all the way up to the roof of the tree house and then down. Go around-up-down. Don't lift your pencil!"

D—"This capital has two strokes. First, start at the top line and make a straight down stroke to the bottom line. Lift your pencil. Back at the top go out-around."

✍ "Draw a dove. Keep your eyes open wide today and try to find a real feather to glue on your drawing."

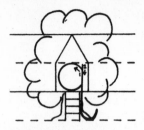

Letter Formation—q & Q

q—"Start this letter like the g. But turn the monkey tail the opposite way. It goes to 4 o'clock [or right]."

Q—"Make a large circle, starting at the 2 o'clock position. Lift your pencil and add a short slanting line."

✍ "The title Queen begins with the letter Q. Find the story of brave Queen Esther in the Bible or your favorite Bible story book. After you hear it again, imagine how beautiful Esther's crown must have been. Draw a crown fit for a queen."

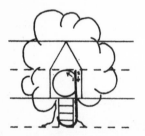

Letter Formation—g & G

g—"Begin at the 2 o'clock position and go around-down with a monkey tail to 8 o'clock [or left]."

G—"Make a C and add a shelf—without lifting your pencil."

✍ "G begins the word go. Can you spell it? Write the word several times. Then draw a traffic light with the green light lit."

Letter Formation—c & C

c—"Begin this letter at 2 o'clock and end at 4 o'clock. It goes up-around. See the open gate?"

C—"Make the capital with exactly the same stroke as the lowercase letter, but make sure it's bigger. The capital letter goes from the top line clear down to the bottom line."

✍ "C begins a word we use a lot—Come. 'Come here.' 'Come help me.' Can you tell someone to come without saying a word, just motioning with your hands? See how many people you can 'talk' to without saying a word."

Letter Formation—e & E

e—"Begin by making a straight line in the middle of the space. Go out-up-around. Don't lift your pencil!"

E—"It takes four strokes to make this capital letter. First, make the long down stroke. Then make three shorter ones, starting at the top of the letter, then the middle, then the bottom. The center side stroke is shorter than the top and bottom ones."

✍ "Write a lot of e's on a page, then add faces and hair to each one. Do your e's look like a bunch of people talking to each other?"

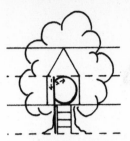

Letter Formation—p & P

p—"This letter is somewhat like the b. But be careful—it has some big differences! It starts at the dotted line and goes down to the bottom of the ladder. The stroke is down-up-around. Don't lift your pencil until you're finished."

P—"The capital begins at the top line. The first stroke is a long down one. Pick up your pencil and again start at the line. Go around to the middle line."

✍ "Draw a picture of your pet, or an animal you'd like to have for a pet. Maybe you'd better draw a cage if your pet is wild!"

Letter Formation—b & B

b—"This letter is like making a bat and attaching a ball right next to it. Begin at the roof and end at the floor. The stroke is down-up-around, without lifting your pencil."

B—"This capital letter has two strokes. First, start at the top line and make a straight down stroke to the bottom line. Lift your pencil. Back at the top go around-around."

✍ "B begins a very special word, Bible. Write it several times. Notice that this word has both a capital and a lowercase b in it. Can you count how many Bibles are in your home or classroom?"

Letter Formation—i & I

i—"Start at the dotted line. The stroke is down. Then put the dot in the middle of the attic."

I—"Start at the top line and go down to the bottom line. For the small cross pieces, go left to right. Do the top one first."

✍ "The ibex is a wild goat. Can someone help you find, in a dictionary or encyclopedia, where the ibex lives and what kind of horns he has? Jesus created many interesting animals for us to enjoy."

Letter Formation—t & T

t—"This letter is different from all others. It is the only letter that begins in the middle of the attic. Make a stick down. Then go across at the dotted line."

T—"Start at the roof and go down to the bottom line. Make a nice cross at the top line, going from left to right."

✍ "There are so many things for which to be thankful! Draw a picture of at least four things you're thankful for."

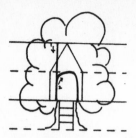

Letter Formation—h & H

h—"Begin this letter at the roof. The stroke is down-up-over. Does this letter remind you of a chair?"

H—"This capital has two side strokes of the same height—from the top line to the bottom line. Then connect them with a bridge across at the dotted line."

✍ "Draw hearts in many sizes and colors. Can you draw several hearts—starting with a big heart with smaller and smaller ones inside?"

Letter Formation—l & L

l—"This is one of the easiest letters. Begin at the top of the roof and make a stick going straight down to the bottom of the meeting room."

L—"Start at the roof and go down to the bottom line. But keep on going! Make a leg for it to stand on, going from left to right."

✍ "The Bible talks about our being lights that should not be hid. Talk about ways that people can be lights. Then draw a picture of some kind of light."

Letter Formation—r & R

r—"Begin at the dotted line. The stroke is down-up-over partway."

R—"Start at the top line and go straight down to the bottom line. Pick up your pencil and at the top, curve around-in-out with a straight leg."

✍ "R begins the word rainbow. Tell someone a Bible story that mentions a rainbow. Then draw a rainbow with the colors in the right order."

Letter Formation—n & N

n—"This letter begins like the r—at the dotted line. The stroke is down-up-around-down. It ends at the bottom line."

N—"Start at the top line and go clear down to the bottom line. Then pick up your pencil. The second long stroke is an angle down-straight up."

✍ "Be nice today and do something helpful for a friend—but don't tell who did it!"

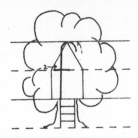

Letter Formation—f & F

f—"Begin at the 2 o'clock position. The stroke is like a cane: up-around-down. Lift your pencil and make a cross at the dotted line."

F—"This capital is similar to the E except that it doesn't have the bottom leg. First, make the long down stroke. Then make two shorter ones, starting at the top. The second one is shorter than the first."

✍ "Draw a basket with at least three kinds of fruit in it."

Letter Formation—m & M

m—"This letter has one more hump than the n. Count the down parts of the stroke: 1-2-3. Down-up-around-down-up-around-down."

M—"This is a difficult capital letter. Listen carefully, because it has only two strokes. Start by making a tall stick from the top line down to the bottom line. The next stroke goes from top to bottom, too, but it changes direction. Go angle down-angle up-straight down."

✍ "Draw a picture for Mom to thank her for something she has done for you in the past week."

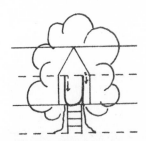

Letter Formation—u & U

u—"Start at the dotted line. The stroke is down-curve around-up-down. Does making this letter remind you of crawling under a fence?"

U—"This capital is made just like the lowercase letter, except that it fills the space from the top line to the bottom line."

✍ "Draw a picture of yourself under an umbrella. Are you smiling because your hair isn't getting wet?"

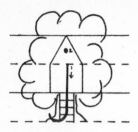

Letter Formation—j & J

j—"Begin this letter at the dotted line. It goes down the ladder to the ground with a monkey tail. Make the stroke this way: down-curve left. Make the dot last. The dot belongs in the middle of the attic."

J—"Start at the top line and go straight down to 4 o'clock, then curve to the left to the 8 o'clock position."

✎ "Do you jump for joy? See how many times you can jump rope without missing or stopping."

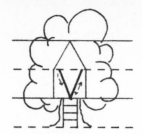

Letter Formation—v & V

v—"It's important not to pick up the pencil when making these letters. This one stays in the meeting room. It starts and ends at the dotted line. The stroke is made angle down-angle up."

V—"The capital is just like the lower-case letter, except that it fills the space from the top line to the bottom line. Make the stroke the same, angle down-angle up."

✎ "In one of His parables, Jesus talks about the vine. Design a vine, making it cover as much of the page as you can. Draw a few birds or bugs hiding in the vine."

Letter Formation—y & Y

y—"This letter also goes from the dotted line to the ground, but it is made with straight lines only. The first stroke is a short one that slants down. Then a longer line that slants the other way and goes clear down the ladder."

Y—"Start this capital by making a v sit on top of the dotted line. The second stroke is a stick that goes on down to the bottom line."

✎ "Yes is a word we need to say often. Practice writing 'yes' and then talk about some questions with 'yes' answers."

Letter Formation—w & W

w—"Here's another letter that stays in the meeting room and is made with just one long stroke. Angle down-angle up-angle down-angle up."

W—"The capital is just like the lowercase letter, only larger. Use one long, smooth stroke to make the letter!"

✎ "Worms are interesting to study. Find out why some worms are useful to gardeners. Use a pipecleaner to make a 'worm.' Wrap the pipecleaner around a pencil, then carefully pull the pencil free. Tie a string to your 'worm' and you have an instant pet to pull around!"

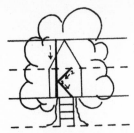

Letter Formation—k & K

k—"Begin this letter at the roof. The first stroke is straight down. Lift your pencil. The next stroke starts at the dotted line and goes slant in-slant out."

K—"This capital is very much like the lowercase letter. The long stick goes from the top line down to the bottom. Lift your pencil after making that stroke. The next stroke starts at the dotted line and goes slant in-slant out."

☞ "K is for the Kingdom where we all want to live someday. Look in Revelation 21:16-21 for a description. Isn't it hard to imagine how beautiful it will be? Can you draw a picture showing some of the gold and precious jewels?"

Letter Formation—x & X

x—"Both strokes in this letter start at the dotted line. The first one is to the left and is a slanted down stroke that ends at the right. Start the second stroke at the right and slant down in the opposite direction."

X—"This is another capital that is formed with the same strokes as its lowercase letter. Just make sure both sticks go from the top line to the bottom line."

☞ "Not many words begin with x. Design an exit sign and put it by a door that goes out of the classroom."

Letter Formation—s & S

s—"This letter just slides along in one smooth stroke. It starts at the 2 o'clock position and curves up-around-down-around-up."

S—"Make a larger version of the lowercase letter for a capital. See how smooth you can make your letter."

☞ "Sing a special song to someone special today!"

Letter Formation—z & Z

z—"This letter starts at the dotted line. But you make it without lifting your pencil. The stroke goes like this: straight line right-slant down toward left-straight line right."

Z—"If you've mastered the lowercase z, then you can also make the capital letter. Use the same zig-zagging stroke, but make it larger."

☞ "Think of the zoo and the animals that live there. Draw a picture of a zebra."

Vocabulary List — "Words of Promise"

This list is composed of the practice words from the lessons.

A
after
all
along
am
and
are

B
be
because
become
before
begin
belongs
blesses
blessing
body
born
brother
burst

C
can
compose
counting

D
day
delight
delights
direct
do
done

E
each
earth
enjoyable
enter
every
everything
evil
except
exciting
exit

F
faithfulness
fall
fear
feet
few
filled
for
forgiveness
founded
friendship
fully

G
get
glad
God
godly
good
greatest

H
hands
harp
have
he
heart
hearts
heart's
heavens
help
hides
higher
him
himself
his
holds
holy
honeycomb
honor
hope
how

I
I
in
is
it

J
joy
joyful
jump
just

K
keep
kind
king
know

L
law
laws
lazy
lead
life
like
Lord
Lord's
love

M
make
man's
me
men
much
my

N
need
never
new
no

O
obey
of
oh
on
once
our

P
paths
plans
poor
praise
promises
Prov.
Psalms
put
puts

Q
quarrel

R
rich
richly
right
rises

S
saves
should
sing
so
someone
song
songs
soon
stop
symphony

T
tell
that
the
thing
those
time
to
trust
truthful

U
undeserving
unless
unmoved
useless

V
vast
vastness

W
wait
walk
what
when
who
wholeheartedly
will
willing
wiser
with
word
words
work
world
wrong

Y
yes
you
your

Z
zip

Skills List Index — "Words of Promise"

These alphabet letters emphasized for practice may be found on the following pages.

Vocabulary List — "Words of Jesus"

This list is composed of the practice words from the lessons.

A
all
always
am
and
angels
are
as
ask
at
away

B
be
big
bless
blessings
book
bring
buzz

C
came
can
care
come
criticize
cross

D
day
didn't
different
do
done
down

E
each
ears
else
end
even
ever
exist
exit

F
face
Father
fill
follow
for
four
free
friend
friendly
from

G
give
go
God
great
guess

H
has
he
hear
heart
heaven
Him
his
holy
home
honest

I
I
if
in
into
is
it

J
jaws
Jesus
joy
jump

K
keep
kind
kingdom
know

L
large
late
light
listen
live
Lord
love

M
make
matters
mind
much
my

N
near
never

O
of
on
only
or
other
others

P
peace
people
play
please
practice
praise
prepared
prize
put

Q
quick
quickly
quit

R
ready
rejoice
repent
return
rich

S
said
Savior
say
Scriptures
set
shall
sin
six
small
so
sure

T
take
that
the
them
then
there
things
those
time
to
tomorrow
too
true
truth
turn

U
unless
up
us
use

W
wait
want
we
what
when
who
will
with
won't
word
words
world
worship

Y
yes
yet
you
your

These alphabet letters emphasized for practice may be found on the following pages.

A
14, 89, **125, 149**

a
14, 17, 19, 43, 47, 89, **112, 119, 149**

N
23, 97, 101, **157, 161**

n
23, 26, 55, 97, 101, **117 119, 157, 161**

B
20, 32, 87, **127, 147**

b
20, 22, 51, 69, 87, **116, 147**

O
14, 32, 71, **125, 149**

o
14, 17, 19, 45, 71, **112, 149**

C
15, 32, 71, 87, **125, 147**

c
15, 17, 19, 49, 71, 87, **112 147**

P
20, 32, 75, 83, **132, 143**

p
20, 22, 51, 75, 83, **113, 143**

D
14, 32, 89, **126, 149**

d
14, 17, 19, 43, 89, **112, 149**

Q
18, 32, 91, **151**

q
18, 22, 47, 91, **113, 151**

E
15, 32, 75, 83, 93, **126, 143, 153**

e
15, 17, 19, 49, 75, 83, 93, **111, 119, 143, 153**

R
21, 32, 99, **132, 159**

r
21, 22, 55, 99, **116, 159**

F
24, 32, 85, 95, **128, 145, 155**

f
24, 26, 85, 95, **115, 145 155**

S
25, 73, **127, 153**

s
25, 26, 65, 73, **116, 153**

G
18, 32, 81, 87, 91, **127, 147, 151**

g
18, 19, 22, 45, 81, 87, 91, **113, 147, 151**

T
16, 32, 81, 101, **128, 161**

t
16, 17, 53, 57, 81, 101, **115, 161**

H
21, 32, 75, 85, **129, 145**

h
21, 22, 67, 75, 85, **111, 145**

U
24, 101, **130, 161**

u
24, 26, 61, 101, **114, 161**

I
16, 32, 97, **128, 143, 157**

i
16, 17, 53, 59, 97, **114, 119, 143, 157**

V
28, 77, **130**

v
28, 31, 61, 77, **117**

J
27, 99, 133, **159**

j
27, 31, 59, 99, **115, 159**

W
28, 73, **129**

w
28, 31, 63, 73, **114**

K
25, 97, **129, 157**

k
25, 26, 67, 97, **111, 157**

X
29, 77, **130, 155**

x
29, 31, 65, 77, **118, 155**

L
16, 32, 79, **133, 159**

l
16, 17, 53, 79, **111, 119, 159**

Y
27, 85, 93, **131, 145, 153**

y
27, 31, 63, 85, 93, **118, 145, 153**

M
23, 95, **155**

m
23, 26, 55, 95, **117, 155**

Z
29, 79, **131, 151**

z
29, 31, 69, 79, **118, 151**

Alphabet Practice
38, 39, **121, 135, 137**

Letter Formation
5, **107**

Spacing
4

Circles & Sticks
9, 10, 11

Numbers
12, 13, **137**

Tree House
3

Homonyms
85

Paper & Pencil Position
5

Dear Friend,

Each week our class writes a Bible verse as part of our handwriting lesson. This week we want to share a verse with you.

We hope you have a good week with God's blessing. We are praying for you.

Love,

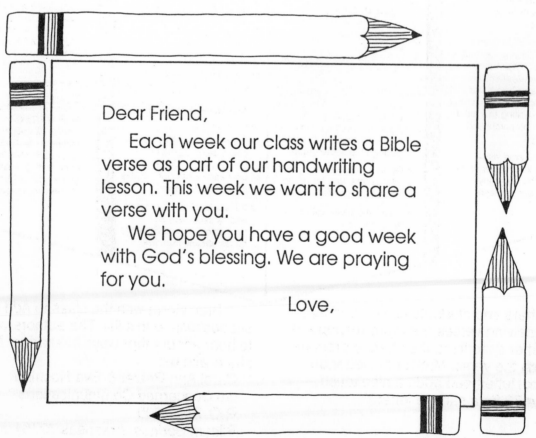

Dear Friend,

Each week our class writes a Bible verse as part of our handwriting lesson. This week we want to share a verse with you.

We hope you have a good week with God's blessing. We are praying for you.

Love,

Ways to Share

Most students enjoy writing their verses on the special Scripture border sheets and then decorating them. But even more, they should find satisfaction in sharing these gems from Scripture.

Sending the verses home with the students can be a real blessing to their families. But for variety, why not sponsor an outreach activity in which the entire class can participate at least once a month?

Here are some suggestions for ways students can share their verses. A classroom should be able to discover several additional ways, too!

Ways to Share:

- Put the verse in a place where members of the family will see it every day. Suggest the door of the refrigerator or a common bulletin board.

- Send the Scripture border sheet to work with a parent to share with fellow employees.

- Give the page to grandparents. (Encourage each student to include a personal message. The student can be given an extra Scripture border sheet to use for writing this letter; these can be purchased separately.)

- Share the verse with someone who works at the school—the secretary, janitor, groundskeeper, or principal.

- Encourage another Christian. (The church secretary could provide names of families in the congregation who would especially appreciate a special Scripture verse of encouragement.)

- If your students want to share their border sheets with a prisoner, you may call Concerned Communications at 1-501-549-9000 for the name & address of a prison ministries group that will forward the verse along with a letter without revealing the sender's address. Replies from the prisoner to the sender will be directed through the same group.

- Go to a nursing home, visit one patient, and leave the verse to decorate the room.

- Share the verse with a neighbor.

- Make a placemat. Center the Scripture border sheet on a large piece of construction paper or a plain paper placemat. Laminate the sheet or cover it with clear contact paper.

- Give the verse to someone who is sick. Hospitals may like to give verses to patients on their breakfast trays.

- Think of someone who is housebound. Deliver the verse in person, if possible.

Additional suggestions for teachers:

- Create an attractive bulletin board using Scripture border sheets. Or select the best each week and display it in a special place.

- If the school has a general display case, ask for permission to post Scripture border sheets from the class.

- See whether a church would like to display the best Scripture border sheets or enclose one with each copy of the church newsletter when it's mailed.

- Get a copy of church members' addresses. Go down the list, sending each family a Scripture border sheet with a personal note. Students will be delighted with the positive response this will generate!

- Send the best samples from the classroom to the publisher of *A REASON FOR WRITING* for possible display at educational conventions. Be sure to label each sheet (on the back) with the name, age, grade, and school of the student who created it.

Teachers and students have found that people receiving verses are more responsive when a letter describing the sharing program is sent with the verse. Mailing the letter on your school letterhead adds a nice touch. (See page 72 for a sample letter.)

Brainstorm with the class to add more suggestions to this list. The authors would like to hear about other ways of sharing. Please share with us!

Carol Ann Retzer & Eva Hoshino
c/o Concerned Communications
P. O. Box 1000
Siloam Springs, Arkansas 72761

Teaching
A Reason For Writing:

Transition

Words of Jesus

Words to Live By

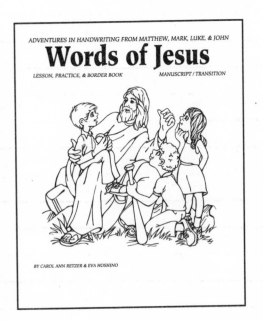

ADVENTURES IN HANDWRITING FROM MATTHEW, MARK, LUKE, & JOHN
Words of Jesus
LESSON, PRACTICE, & BORDER BOOK   MANUSCRIPT / TRANSITION

BY CAROL ANN RETZER & EVA HOSHINO

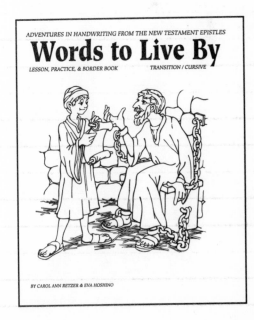

ADVENTURES IN HANDWRITING FROM THE NEW TESTAMENT EPISTLES
Words to Live By
LESSON, PRACTICE, & BORDER BOOK   TRANSITION / CURSIVE

BY CAROL ANN RETZER & EVA HOSHINO

Cursive Letter Formation

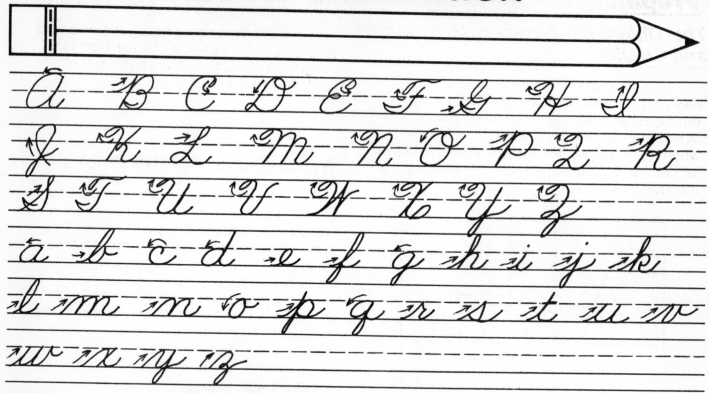

Manuscript Letter Formation

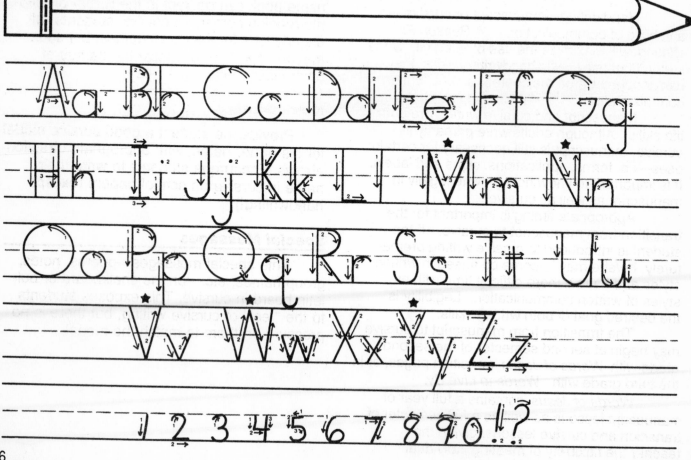

Preparing Students for Transition to Cursive Writing

The Difference Between Manuscript and Cursive

The word **cursive** comes from a word meaning "to run." And in cursive the letters **do** run together to form a word. Just as a person doesn't run standing straight up, so letters, when run together, will slant. Naturally, cursive letters are formed somewhat differently than manuscript letters.

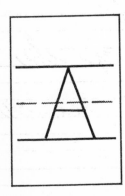 

Timing for Beginning Transition to Cursive Writing

Handwriting—manuscript or cursive—is a vehicle of communication. *A Reason For Writing* will maximize the use of this skill. Once students master basic handwriting skills, they can concentrate on the content of their written communication.

Manuscript and cursive writing are both life skills. Although adults write primarily in cursive, manuscript is still necessary for certain uses—i.e. forms, applications, signs and labels. It is important to know how to write legibly in manuscript as well as cursive.

Appropriate timing is important for the transition from manuscript to cursive. If the student is introduced to cursive writing prematurely, he/she may become confused in writing styles and have a more difficult time with all styles of written communication. Legibility is the desired goal of both writing skills.

The transition from manuscript to cursive may begin at second semester of the second grade with *Words of Jesus* transition pages, or in the third grade with *Words to Live By.*

Words of Jesus contains a full year of manuscript lessons as well as a full semester of transition and cursive lessons, giving the teacher the flexibility of meeting individual needs. If the transition is begun in the second grade, the students will still benefit from the cursive practice pages at the beginning of *Words to Live By.*

Readiness for Cursive Writing

Visual readiness activities can provide cursive readiness experiences that will pave the way for successful writing experiences. You can build on students' natural enthusiasm for moving on to cursive writing by giving them visual readiness.

Here are several specific activities to provide visual readiness for successful cursive writing experiences.

Class Name Book

On 4 x 6 cards write, in cursive, the name of each student in the class. Punch the cards and put them together on a ring. The class name book can be kept in the library or favorite reading corner. Of course, students will eagerly look for their own names, but soon they will begin to recognize the names of other class members as well.

Name Writing

Provide the student a good cursive model for his or her name, with appropriate direction arrows. Encourage students to write their name in cursive on school papers (except handwriting!).

Special Messages

Write special messages—poems, notes, group names, etc.—on the chalkboard or bulletin board in cursive. This exposes students to the "feel" of cursive writing, but there is no pressure on them to match the model.

Alphabet Puzzle Cards

Cut strips of paper into matching pairs *(see sample drawing)*. Write the manuscript letter on one and the corresponding cursive letter on the other. The matching ends provide a self-check for the student. These cards are an excellent addition for a learning center and can be used individually or by a small group.

Word Puzzle Cards

Make the same kind of matching-pair cards as for the activity above, using words instead of letters. These could be the new reading words for the day, the spelling words, or even the words from the handwriting lesson.

Manuscript	Cursive
A a	*A a*
D d	*D d*
G g	*G g*
B b	*B b*

Manuscript	Cursive
cap	*cap*
boy	*boy*
sun	*sun*
hat	*hat*

Transition Instruction

Often not enough time is spent on actual transition instruction. It's not a stage of growth that will happen automatically. Transition will take place with fewer problems if students have been prepared visually and have the necessary motor skills.

Students will be eager to begin cursive writing. When the teacher feels the student has mastered manuscript writing sufficiently, and is ready to begin cursive writing, the transition *Student Workbooks* (**Words of Jesus** and **Words to Live By**) provide the necessary transition exercises. The exercises will take from six to eight weeks to complete, depending upon the amount of work assigned. Most students can easily do a page a day.

Introduce the letter and provide adequate time for practice. Be alert to any difficulty a student may be having, and plan for additional review and practice in specific strokes and letters. The letters are introduced with similar stroke letters. This makes it easier for the student to get the letter patterns well in mind. At any time a student is having difficulty with a certain letter, it is helpful to review the letter group (as shown on page 81 and 82).

The first practice pages in the *Student Workbooks* are for review and comparison. Discuss with students the similarities and differences between the manuscript and cursive alphabets. Manuscript letters and words are written in the introduction pages to give the visual carry-over from manuscript to cursive writing. Remind students that they will find many uses for the manuscript writing and should plan to keep it for a life skill.

Discuss and describe the formation of each basic stroke and letter. Since students learn in different modalities, the teacher should cover all aspects in the introduction of each letter. Here is a suggested sequence:

✎ Name and describe the letter (auditory):
"The letter for today is **d**. The letter begins like an **o**. Go around-up-and trace back down to the baseline."

✎ Move with the letter (kinesthetic).
Skywrite the letter. Using the pointer finger of your writing hand, make the letter motion in the air. Then use the pointer finger of your writing hand to form the letter on the palm of your other hand.

✎ Write the letter (visual).
Let the student practice on the chalkboard as well as on paper.

Vary the method of introduction so it doesn't become too routine, but take care to describe thoroughly each letter.

Sample suggested letter descriptions are included for selected letters. However, students' own descriptions will probably become more meaningful to them.

Suggested Weekly Program Using the Lesson Section

Day 1

- Read the Verse of the Week aloud.
- Introduce the practice letter or letters.
- Read aloud the tips at the top of the page.
- Students should complete the practice section for the day.

Day 2

- Read the Verse of the Week aloud.
- Read aloud the words for practice.
- Students should complete the practice section for the day.

Day 3

- Read the Verse of the Week aloud.
- The teacher should review the tips, and students should evaluate their progress.
- Students should complete the practice section for the day.
- The teacher should remind students that this lesson is the final word practice for the week. Each student should ask, "Are there areas where I may be having difficulty?" The teacher should be available to monitor individual students for correct letter formation.

Day 4

- Read the Verse of the Week aloud.
- Students should practice writing the verse at least once on penmanship paper.
- Students should choose a Scripture border sheet from the back of the book.   Encourage them to do their best writing of the week on the Scripture border sheet.

Day 5

- Read the Verse of the Week aloud.
- Students should decorate their Scripture border sheets.
- Students should discuss what they can do with their completed verses. (See "Ways to Share," page 89.)

Suggestion: Make notes and suggestions on the students' **practice** work. If you want to make a positive comment about the final verse, write it on a peel-off note so that the Scripture border sheet is always appropriate for sharing.

80

Practicing for Speed

Although speed is not the main concern of handwriting practice, some students need to work at increasing their speed. The simple exercise given below will help you to evaluate how students are performing:

Choose one of the sentences in bold below and use it throughout the exercise. Have students write the sentence as many times as they can in one minute. Then allow a one-minute rest. Students should write the sentence for a second minute; rest a minute. Finally, students should write the sentence for a third minute. Count the number of letters written.

This exercise should be tried first for quality, then for speed. Keep a record for each child and compare his progress throughout the year. Here are three good sentences that contain 20 letters each:

✎ **Writing for speed is fun.**

✎ **She will meet you at home.**

✎ **Write all papers neatly.**

Connective Strokes for Practice

Letter Groups for Lowercase Letters

There are three basic strokes in cursive writing: the **undercurve**, the **overcurve**, and the **downcurve**. You can teach these basic beginning strokes through three letter forms: **i, n**, and **a**. After you have introduced these beginning strokes, students are ready to learn the categories of lowercase letters.

There are five categories or groups of lowercase cursive letters:

Upper Loop Letters— e, l, b, h, k

General instruction: Start on the baseline and make an undercurve line. Make a loop like a lasso, return to the baseline, and swing up slightly.

Downcurve or Oval Letters— a, d, g, q, o, c

o: Starting at the 2 o'clock position, make a slanted oval, and add a checkstroke.

Checkstroke is a helpful term for students to learn. It is the short retrace and right motion that makes the ending stroke on cursive letters **o, v, w**, and **b**.

d: Make an oval, then go straight up. Stop and retrace the slanted straight line down to the baseline, and finish with a connecting stroke.

Undercurve Letters— i, u, j, s, r, w, f, t

i: Start at the baseline and curve upward. Stop at the dotted line and retrace down halfway before curving out to the baseline. Dot.

Overcurve Letters— m, n, v, y, x, z

m: Start at the baseline and make an overcurved line back to the baseline, go right back up again, and again once more, then end with a connecting stroke.

Lower Loop Letters—
p, q, j, y, z, g, f

With the exception of the **p**, these letters are all contained in another group. They are in this group because they all have a characteristic lower loop as well.

p: Start at the baseline and curve upward. Stop. Make a straight slanted line down below the baseline. Form a loop and make an oval on the baseline. Swing out with the connecting stroke.

p, q, j, y, z, g, f

Cursive Capitals

One additional stroke is used for capitals—the cane-stem stroke. The cane-stem is the small loop near the top line that begins the capital. The stroke resembles a walking cane, and it is most easily identifiable in the **H**.

Most of the capital letters fall into general stroke groups as well. These are helpful for introducing the letters and also for continuing practice.

Oval Group—
O, C, E, A, D

O, C, E, A, D

Boat Endings—
B, I, G, S, T, F

B, I, G, S, T, F

Cane-stem Stroke Group—
H, K, M, N, W, X, U, V, Y, Q, Z

H, K, M, N, W, X, U, V, Y, Q, Z

Upper Loop Letters—
L, J

L, J

Once the letters have all been presented and practiced, students are ready for the verse lessons. Each lesson is broken down into sections for each day of the week. On the following page is a suggested schedule to follow for the remainder of the school year.

Sentence Evaluation

The sentence on the pencil contains all the letters of the alphabet. It is good to use for an overall evalution of handwriting. Ask students to write the sentence at the beginning of the grading period and again at the end. Any specific letter problems students have should show up in this sentence evaluation.

Grading

For evaluation, keep a folder of samples for each student, with pages from the beginning and ending of each grading period. When it's time to give grades, you can evaluate each student **on his or her own progress**. If the student is regularly taking home Scripture border sheets, parents should be aware of their child's handwriting improvement.

Some teachers have found the 10-point grading scale (below) helpful. It covers all 5 areas for evaluation and allows students to know exactly how they will be evaluated. (Please see page 109 for a Black-line master for duplication and use in your classroom.)

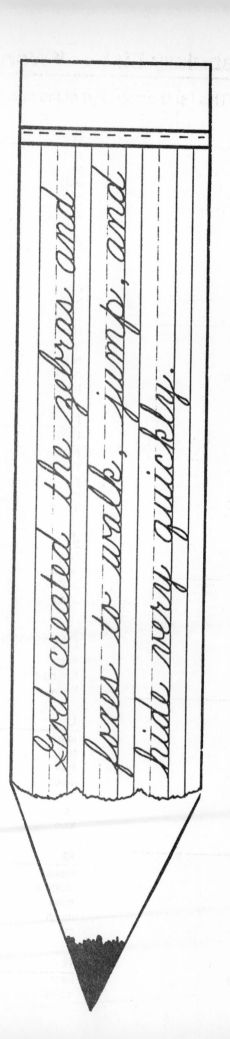

Handwriting Evaluation Form

2 points possible for each:

Alignment
Letter stays on the line.   _____

Slant
Letters have the same slant.   _____

Size
Capital and lowercase letters
are the right size.   _____

Shape
Letters are shaped correctly
and neatly.   _____

Spacing
Letters and words are spaced
and spelled correctly.   _____

                              TOTAL   _____

Vocabulary List — "Words of Jesus"

This list is composed of the practice words from the lessons.

A
all
always
am
and
angels
are
as
ask
at
away

B
be
big
bless
blessings
book
bring
buzz

C
came
can
care
come
criticize
cross

D
day
didn't
different
do
done
down

E
each
ears
else
end
even
ever
exist
exit

F
face
Father
fill
follow
for
four
free
friend
friendly
from

G
give
go
God
great
guess

H
has
he
hear
heart
heaven
Him
his
holy
home
honest

I
I
if
in
into
is
it

J
jaws
Jesus
joy
jump

K
keep
kind
kingdom
know

L
large
late
light
listen
live
Lord
love

M
make
matters
mind
much
my

N
near
never

O
of
on
only
or
other
others

P
peace
people
play
please
practice
praise
prepared
prize
put

Q
quick
quickly
quit

R
ready
rejoice
repent
return
rich

S
said
Savior
say
Scriptures
set
shall
sin
six
small
so
sure

T
take
that
the
them
then
there
things
those
time
to
tomorrow
too
true
truth
turn

U
unless
up
us
use

W
wait
want
we
what
when
who
will
with
won't
word
words
world
worship

Y
yes
yet
you
your

Skills List Index — "Words of Jesus"

Manuscript/ **Transition**

These alphabet letters emphasized for practice may be found on the following pages.

A
14, 89, **125, 149**

a
14, 17, 19, 43, 47, 89, **112, 119, 149**

N
23, 97, 101, **157, 161**

n
23, 26, 55, 97, 101, **117 119, 157, 161**

B
20, 32, 87, **127, 147**

b
20, 22, 51, 69, 87, **116, 147**

O
14, 32, 71, **125, 149**

o
14, 17, 19, 45, 71, **112, 149**

C
15, 32, 71, 87, **125, 147**

c
15, 17, 19, 49, 71, 87, **112 147**

P
20, 32, 75, 83, **132, 143**

p
20, 22, 51, 75, 83, **113, 143**

D
14, 32, 89, **126, 149**

d
14, 17, 19, 43, 89, **112, 149**

Q
18, 32, 91, **151**

q
18, 22, 47, 91, **113, 151**

E
15, 32, 75, 83, 93, **126, 143, 153**

e
15, 17, 19, 49, 75, 83, 93, **111, 119, 143, 153**

R
21, 32, 99, **132, 159**

r
21, 22, 55, 99, **116, 159**

F
24, 32, 85, 95, **128, 145, 155**

f
24, 26, 85, 95, **115, 145 155**

S
25, 73, **127, 153**

s
25, 26, 65, 73, **116, 153**

G
18, 32, 81, 87, 91, **127, 147, 151**

g
18, 19, 22, 45, 81, 87, 91, **113, 147, 151**

T
16, 32, 81, 101, **128, 161**

t
16, 17, 53, 57, 81, 101, **115, 161**

H
21, 32, 75, 85, **129, 145**

h
21, 22, 67, 75, 85, **111, 145**

U
24, 101, **130, 161**

u
24, 26, 61, 101, **114, 161**

I
16, 32, 97, **128, 143, 157**

i
16, 17, 53, 59, 97, **114, 119, 143, 157**

V
28, 77, **130**

v
28, 31, 61, 77, **117**

J
27, 99, 133, **159**

j
27, 31, 59, 99, **115, 159**

W
28, 73, **129**

w
28, 31, 63, 73, **114**

K
25, 97, **129, 157**

k
25, 26, 67, 97, **111, 157**

X
29, 77, **130, 155**

x
29, 31, 65, 77, **118, 155**

L
16, 32, 79, **133, 159**

l
16, 17, 53, 79, **111, 119, 159**

Y
27, 85, 93, **131, 145, 153**

y
27, 31, 63, 85, 93, **118, 145, 153**

M
23, 95, **155**

m
23, 26, 55, 95, **117, 155**

Z
29, 79, **131, 151**

z
29, 31, 69, 79, **118, 151**

Alphabet Practice
38, 39, **121, 135, 137**

Letter Formation
5, **107**

Spacing
4

Circles & Sticks
9, 10, 11

Numbers
12, 13, **137**

Tree House
3

Homonyms
85

Paper & Pencil Position
5

Vocabulary List — "Words to Live By"

This list is composed of the practice words from the lessons.

A

abilities
again
ago
all
allowance
always
and
another

B

be
beautiful
because
become
before
belong
bless
bring
but

C

charm
children
chose
Christ
Christian
church
citizens
comes
coming
continue
control
country
courteous

D

dear
deep
delights
doing
done
don't
down

E

each
earnest
even
every
everything
evil
example

F

family
Father
faults
fellowship
following
for
forgave
forgive
friends
full

G

gentle
gentleness
gifts
give
given
glad
glory
God
God's
good
great
grudges
guard
guide

H

happens
happy
harmony
has
have
he
hearts
heaven
help
helping
his
home
household
humble

I

if
important
in
inside
is
it

J

Jesus
John
joy

K

keep
kind

L

lasting
life
light
lips
listening
lives
living
long
Lord
love
loved
loving

M

made
make
makes
making
man
marvelous
may
members
more
most

N

never
new

O

obey
opportunity
other
others

P

patient
peace
perfect
planned
power
praise
pray
prayer
prayers
precious
presence

Q

quiet

R

ready
really
rejoice
remember
repay
results
righteous
roots

S

should
show
snap
soil
some
soon
special
spirit
sure
sympathy

T

telling
tender
thanks
the
their
them
then
those
toward
trust

U

understand
unkind
use

V

very

W

want
watching
what
whatever
which
who
whole
will
wisdom
within
wonderful
work
world

Y

you
your

Skills List Index — "Words to Live By"

These alphabet letters emphasized for practice may be found on the following pages.

Ways to Share

Most students enjoy writing their verses on the special Scripture border sheets and then decorating them. But even more, they should find satisfaction in sharing these gems from Scripture.

Sending the verses home with the students can be a real blessing to their families. But for variety, why not sponsor an outreach activity in which the entire class can participate at least once a month?

Here are some suggestions for ways students can share their verses. A classroom should be able to discover several additional ways, too!

Ways to Share:

- Put the verse in a place where members of the family will see it every day. Suggest the door of the refrigerator or a common bulletin board.

- Send the Scripture border sheet to work with a parent to share with fellow employees.

- Give the page to grandparents. (Encourage each student to include a personal message. The student can be given an extra Scripture border sheet to use for writing this letter; these can be purchased separately.)

- Share the verse with someone who works at the school—the secretary, janitor, groundskeeper, or principal.

- Encourage another Christian. (The church secretary could provide names of families in the congregation who would especially appreciate a special Scripture verse of encouragement.)

- If your students want to share their border sheets with a prisoner, you may call Concerned Communications at 1-501-549-9000 for the name & address of a prison ministries group that will forward the verse along with a letter without revealing the sender's address. Replies from the prisoner to the sender will be directed through the same group.

- Go to a nursing home, visit one patient, and leave the verse to decorate the room.

- Share the verse with a neighbor.

- Make a placemat. Center the Scripture border sheet on a large piece of construction paper or a plain paper placemat. Laminate the sheet or cover it with clear contact paper.

- Give the verse to someone who is sick. Hospitals may like to give verses to patients on their breakfast trays.

- Think of someone who is housebound. Deliver the verse in person, if possible.

Additional suggestions for teachers:

- Create an attractive bulletin board using Scripture border sheets. Or select the best each week and display it in a special place.

- If the school has a general display case, ask for permission to post Scripture border sheets from the class.

- See whether a church would like to display the best Scripture border sheets or enclose one with each copy of the church newsletter when it's mailed.

- Get a copy of church members' addresses. Go down the list, sending each family a Scripture border sheet with a personal note. Students will be delighted with the positive response this will generate!

- Send the best samples from the classroom to the publisher of *A REASON FOR WRITING* for possible display at educational conventions. Be sure to label each sheet (on the back) with the name, age, grade, and school of the student who created it.

Teachers and students have found that people receiving verses are more responsive when a letter describing the sharing program is sent with the verse. Mailing the letter on your school letterhead adds a nice touch. (See page 72 for a sample letter.)

Brainstorm with the class to add more suggestions to this list. The authors would like to hear about other ways of sharing. Please share with us!

Carol Ann Retzer & Eva Hoshino
c/o Concerned Communications
P. O. Box 1000
Siloam Springs, Arkansas 72761

Teaching
A Reason For Writing:

Cursive

Words of Love

Words of Praise

Words of Wisdom

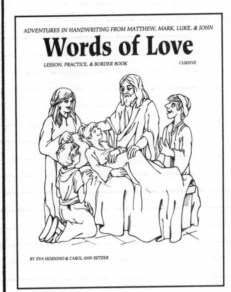

ADVENTURES IN HANDWRITING FROM MATTHEW, MARK, LUKE, & JOHN

Words of Love

LESSON, PRACTICE, & BORDER BOOK   CURSIVE

BY EVA HOSHINO & CAROL ANN RETZER

ADVENTURES IN HANDWRITING FROM PSALMS & PROVERBS

Words of Praise

LESSON, PRACTICE & BORDER BOOK   CURSIVE

BY EVA HOSHINO & CAROL ANN RETZER

ADVENTURES IN HANDWRITING FROM PROVERBS

Words of Wisdom

LESSON, PRACTICE, & BORDER BOOK   CURSIVE

BY EVA HOSHINO & CAROL ANN RETZER

Cursive Letter Formation

Getting Ready to Write

✎ Be comfortable. Clear other books and papers off your desk. Sit well back in the chair with your feet flat on the floor. Your eyes should not be too close to the paper—10-15 inches is ideal.

✎ Hold the pencil correctly. *(See the drawing at the front of your handwriting book.)*

✎ Keep your wrist straight, allowing your arm to move freely.

✎ Place your writing paper at an angle. *(See the drawing at the front of your handwriting book.)*

✎ Take enough time to write neatly.

✎ Work to make your letters the right size. Remember that all small letters should come to the middle dotted line. Capitals should be the same size—from the top line to the bottom line.

✎ Have a good attitude. Be positive about handwriting.

✎ Practice doing your very best.

Note: These suggestions for the student can be posted or duplicated at the discretion of the teacher.

Teaching Cursive Writing

Cursive writing is a necessary form of written communication. It does not come with age maturity but is a learned motor skill. Because many students are not visual learners, they need more than just a model to improve their writing. They will benefit from practice and verbal description of letter size or formation.

Because cursive leter formation has already been introduced by the time a student reaches grades four to six, one might suppose that further instruction is not needed. Books do not teach handwriting—teachers do! SMILE!

Following the **suggested weekly schedule**, the teacher will want to review correct letter formation for the letter or letters of the week. The lessons are designed to take ten to fifteen minutes a day. The benefit of the weekly schedule is that time does not need to be spent explaining format, once the students are in the routine.

Letting students do the entire lesson in one sitting can be counter-productive as it is the daily practice that brings results. It is the quality of the practice—not the quantity.

When students are made aware of the five main points of handwriting evaluation, their work may improve. It is always helpful to let students know what is expected, particularly in terms of neat and legible handwriting. It is amazing the improvement that can be realized when a specific problem can be pinpointed, such as poor alignment, too tight spacing, or letters not filling the space.

If there is a specific letter or letter group a student is having difficulty with, refer to the letter groupings for additional practice (pages 99, 100) and to the connective strokes of different letters. When a student is having trouble with a specific letter, it is good to have him/her practice that letter in groups of six letters. (See p. 80) The practice of the letter, as well as of the connective stroke, is beneficial.

Chalkboard practice in small groups is great, not only for practice, but to easily spot students with incorrect letter formation. Even air-writing with the pointer finger of your writing hand with the students will provide practice to help implant the letter formation in the mind.

There is no substitute for specific remediation to improve handwriting skills when a student is exhibiting a pattern in letter formation that needs correction. It is surprising how quickly one can see results when a specific area for practice is remediated.

The black line masters are helpful for this practice as the lines are the same as in the handwriting books.

For variety in teaching and to keep the student's skills sharpened, occasionally have the students write the verse in manuscript. It is important that they follow the same five guidelines (alignment, slant, size, shape of letters, and spacing) for quality writing.

The decorated border sheets make beautiful bulletin boards. When the students see their work displayed, it does encourage neat work. Also, when a student knows that his/her verses will be sent to someone, or used in sharing as suggested on page 107, the quality of writing will often improve.

Suggested Weekly Schedule

Day 1

- Read the Verse of the Week aloud.
- Introduce the practice letter or letters.
- Read aloud the tips at the top of the page.
- Students should complete the practice section for the day.

Day 2

- Read the Verse of the Week aloud.
- Read aloud the words for practice.
- Students should complete the practice section for the day.

Day 3

- Read the Verse of the Week aloud.
- The teacher should review the tips, and students should evaluate their progress.
- Students should complete the practice section for the day.
- The teacher should remind students that this lesson is the final word practice for the week. Each student should ask, "Are there areas where I may be having difficulty?" The teacher should be available to monitor individual students for correct letter formation.

Day 4

- Read the Verse of the Week aloud.
- Students should practice writing the verse at least once on penmanship paper.
- Students should choose a Scripture border sheet from the back of the book. Encourage them to do their best writing of the week on the Scripture border sheet.

Day 5

- Read the Verse of the Week aloud.
- Students should decorate their Scripture border sheets.
- Students should discuss what they can do with their completed verses. (See "Ways to Share," page 107.)

Suggestion: Make notes and suggestions on the students' **practice** work. If you want to make a positive comment about the final verse, write it on a peel-off note so that the Scripture border sheet is always appropriate for sharing.

LESSON 33

Remember that g, q, p, and f go below the baseline. Make sure that the tall loops are open.

Can others get a good idea of what's in your heart? Do you give them clues by your speech and deeds?

DAY 1
Aa
good
deeds
heart

DAY 2
Gg
wickedness
hidden
produces

DAY 3
Ww
Whatever
overflows
speech

DAY 4
A good man produces good deeds from a good heart. And an evil man produces evil deeds from his hidden wickedness. Whatever is in the heart overflows into speech.
Luke 6:45

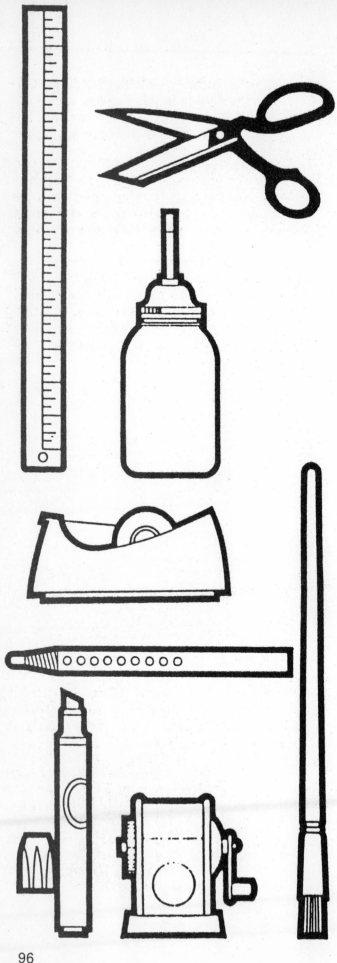

Extended Activities For Cursive Writing

As students become proficient in cursive writing, you can furnish extended activities that provide enjoyable and challenging writing practice.

✏ Children can make lovely original thank-you notes; cards for birthdays, holidays, and other special occasions; invitations; letters to friends and family; pen-pal messages; and posters. A writing center where students can create special messages after their regular work is completed will encourage children to improve their handwriting. You can place items such as these in the writing center: unusual wrapping or construction paper, old greeting cards, stickers, special felt pens, scissors, glue, transparent tape, and yarn or ribbons. You may also want to include some suggested messages, poems, or Scripture verses students can copy into their creations.

✏ Vocabulary lists for each of the Student Workbooks are on pages 101-105. You may wish to assign students to write sentences using words from one of the lists.

✏ Older students may wish to look up in a reference book information about the Verse of the Week. In a Bible commentary they could discover who wrote that book of the Bible, as well as information about the verse. In a paragraph or short essay, students could summarize their findings.

Evaluation of Cursive Writing

You should not insist that each student's slant in cursive writing match either yours or the model's. However, you should remind students that they should strive to write consistently from page to page and from day to day. Occasionally remind students to dot **i**'s and cross **t**'s after completing words.

Stress **quality** in handwriting rather than **quantity**. Each day's practice is short, but you should continually emphasize that mastery will come if students concentrate on each daily practice session.

Here are five areas to look at when evaluating cursive handwriting (please turn to page 61 for a suggested Handwriting Evaluation Form):

✎ **Alignment:** Each letter should sit on the line, not above or below it.

✎ **Slant:** The slant should be uniform. A simple guideline: all down strokes should be made like the number 1.

✎ **Size:** Capital letters are all one full space tall. The lowercase **b**, **d**, **g**, **h**, **k**, and **l** are also one full space tall. The lowercase **t** is about ¾ space tall. All the other lowercase letters are ½ space tall. Letters that go below the line should extend one-half space.

✎ **Shape of letters:** Letters should be consistent and easy to read. Allow some deviation from the model, but insist that letters be formed with the proper strokes.

✎ **Spacing:** Letters should not run into each other, but should be clearly identifiable. Each word should be separated from the next word. A little more space is needed between sentences than between words.

When students understand these points and consistently practice self-analysis on their handwriting, they are able to carry over what they learn in handwriting class to other writing. Encourage this crossover to take place. Good handwriting can help instill pride and self-confidence in each student.

Sentence Evaluation

The sentence on the pencil contains all the letters of the alphabet. It is good to use for an overall evalution of handwriting. Ask students to write the sentence at the beginning of the grading period and again at the end. Any specific letter problems students have should show up in this sentence evaluation.

Grading

For evaluation, keep a folder of samples for each student, with pages from the beginning and ending of each grading period. When it's time to give grades, you can evaluate each student **on his or her own progress**. If the student is regularly taking home Scripture border sheets, parents should be aware of their child's handwriting improvement.

Some teachers have found the 10-point grading scale (below) helpful. It covers all 5 areas for evaluation and allows students to know exactly how they will be evaluated. (Please see page 109 for a Black-line Master for duplication and use in your classroom.)

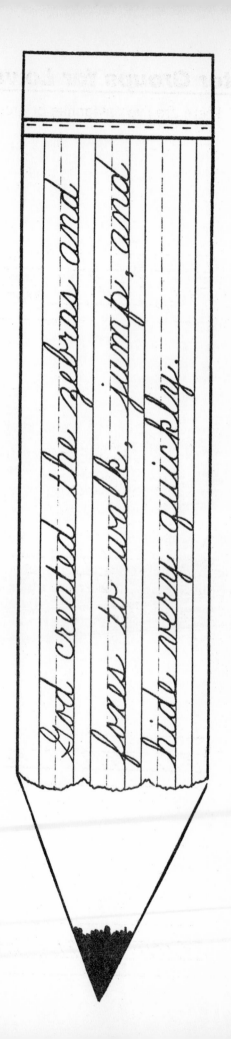

Handwriting Evaluation Form

2 points possible for each:

Alignment
Letter stays on the line. _____

Slant
Letters have the same slant. _____

Size
Capital and lowercase letters
are the right size. _____

Shape
Letters are shaped correctly
and neatly. _____

Spacing
Letters and words are spaced
and spelled correctly. _____

TOTAL _____

Letter Groups for Lowercase Letters

There are five categories or groups of lower-case cursive letters:

Upper Loop Letters—
e, l, b, h, k

General instruction: Start on the baseline and make an undercurve line. Make a loop like a lasso, return to the baseline, and swing up slightly.

e, l, b, h, k

Downcurve or Oval Letters—
a, d, g, q, o, c

o: Starting at the 2 o'clock position, make a slanted oval, and add a checkstroke.

Checkstroke is a helpful term for students to learn. It is the short retrace and right motion that makes the ending stroke on cursive letters **o**, **v**, **w**, and **b**.

d: Make an oval, then go straight up. Stop and retrace the slanted straight line down to the baseline, and finish with a connecting stroke.

a, d, g, q, o, c

Undercurve Letters—
i, u, j, s, r, w, f, t

i: Start at the baseline and curve upward. Stop at the dotted line and retrace down halfway before curving out to the baseline. Dot.

i, u, j, s, r, w, f, t,

Overcurve Letters—
m, n, v, y, x, z

m: Start at the baseline and make an overcurved line back to the baseline, go right back up again, and again once more, then end with a connecting stroke.

m, n, v, y, x, z

Lower Loop Letters—
p, q, j, y, z, g, f

With the exception of the **p**, these letters are all contained in another group. They are in this group because they all have a characteristic lower loop as well.

p: Start at the baseline and curve upward. Stop. Make a straight slanted line down below the baseline. Form a loop and make an oval on the baseline. Swing out with the connecting stroke.

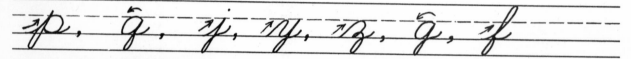

Cursive Capitals

One additional stroke is used for capitals—the cane-stem stroke. The cane-stem is the small loop near the top line that begins the capital. The stroke resembles a walking cane, and it is most easily identifiable in the **H**.

Most of the capital letters fall into general stroke groups as well. These are helpful for introducing the letters and also for continuing practice.

Oval Group—
O, C, E, A, D

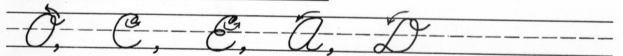

Boat Endings—
B, I, G, S, T, F

Cane-stem Stroke Group—
H, K, M, N, W, X, U, V, Y, Q, Z

Upper Loop Letters—
L, J

Vocabulary List — "Words of Love"

This list is composed of the practice words from the lessons.

A

about
against
all
alone
always
and
anyone
anyway
asking
away

B

back
baptized
be
because
before
behind
believe
believes
birds
blessed
blessings
branch
builds
but

C

cannot
care
caring
cheat
cheer
child
come
Comforter
commandment
condemn
corners
criticize
criticized
curse

D

dark
darkness
deeds
dens
disciples
do
don't
door
down

E

earth
earthly
easy
enemies
enter
eternal
even
everyone
everywhere
evil
exactly
except
extinguish

F

face
Father
feeds
filled
finding
flavor
floodlight
follow
food
for
forgive
foxes
friends
fruitful

G

getting
gift
giving
God
God's
good
greater
greatest
greatness
grudge

H

happiness
hate
haven't
head
heart
hearted
heaven
heavenly
hidden
hides
him
his
holding
Holy Spirit
honest
house

I

I
if
implore
instead
instructions
it

J

Jesus
just

K

keep
knock
knows

L

lamp
lampstand
large
lays
life
light
listen
little
live
living
look
looking
love
loved

M

mankind
man's
many
matters
me
means
measure
Messiah
mind
much
must
my

N

name
need
nests
never
news
no
nor

O

obey
only
opened
other
others
overcome
overflowing
overflows

P

path
peace
perish
person
place
pray
prayer
praying
preach
pressed
produce
produces
prove
puts

R

radiant
real
reap
related
remember
responsibilities
return
reveals
reward
rich
rock
room
running

S

salt
saltiness
same
saved
season
secretly
served
shaken
sheep
shepherd
shines
shown
shut
sins
small
so
solid
Son
soul
source
sow
speech
strength
strong
stumbling

T

take
takes
tell
than
the
them
they
those
though
through
together
told
treasures
treat
trials
truth

U

unless

V

valuable
venom
vine

W

way
welcomes
welcoming
what
whatever
when
who
whoever
wickedness
will
wise
wishing
within
won't
world
worry
worthless

Y

you
your
yourself

Skills List Index — "Words of Love"

These alphabet letters emphasized for practice may be found on the following pages.

Vocabulary List — "Words of Praise"

This list is composed of the practice words from the lessons.

A

above
all
alone
altar
always
answer
are
awesome

B

be
because
been
before
behind
beyond
bless
blows
brave
builders'
builds
but

C

can
caring
cheer
chosen
circumstance
city
clap
clean
come
commit
constant
courageous
create
crumble
cry

D

day
days
defender
delighted
desirable
desires
dishonesty
distress
done
don't
doubts
dripping

E

earth
enemies
enemy
eternal
even
evening
everlasting
every
everyone
everything
evil
exceeding
except

F

faithfulness
fall
fear
feet
few
filled
for
forgiveness
founded
friendship
fully

G

glory
God
God's
gold
good
great
guide

H

hands
harp
have
he
heart
hearts
heart's
heavens
help
hides
higher
him
himself
his
holds
holy
honeycomb
honor
hope
how

I

I
I'll
impatient
instead
is

J

Jehovah
joy
just
justice

K

keep
keeps
kind
kindness

L

laws
lead
let
lifting
listen
live
lives
living
long
longings
Lord
love
lying

M

majesty
may
me
mercy
morning
mount
mountains
my

N

name
near
need
never
night
nothing
number

O

obey
of
oh
on
one
or
other
others
our
overlook

P

path
people
perfect
pillars
point
pour
power
practice
praise
praises
prayed
prayer
preserves
promises
prosper
protection
protects
prove
pure

Q

quick
quiet

R

reach
recognize
refuge
rejoice
renewed
reserved
reverence
right
righteousness
roar
rulers

S

safety
salvation
satisfied
save
sea
secrets
sentries
shares
should
shout
show
sing
sins
skies
so
spend
stand
steady
stouthearted
strength
strong
stumble
success
supreme
sweeter

T

teach
tell
tender
tested
than
thank
that
the
them
then
there
they
think
thinking
those
thoughts
throne
through
time
triumphant
true
trust
turmoil
two

U

undeserving
unless
unmoved
useless

V

vast
vastness

W

wait
walk
what
when
who
wholeheartedly
will
willing
wiser
with
word
words
work
world
wrong

Y

you
your
youthful

Z

Zion

Skills List Index — "Words of Praise"

These alphabet letters emphasized for practice may be found on the following pages.

Vocabulary List — "Words of Wisdom"

This list is composed of the practice words from the lessons.

A

able
acts
advice
always
and
answer
ants
army
away
axe

B

back
basic
be
become
begin
better
blessings
bones
born
break
broken
brother
but

C

careful
character
cheerful
child
choose
chooses
common
completely
conceited
control
corrects
crown
cruel

D

danger
delight
despise
destroyed
direct
dirty
discouragement
does
don't

E

eat
eating
efforts
enemies
energy
enjoyable
enjoys
esteem
even
every
everyone
everything
evil

F

face
fact
famous
father
favor
fear
feather
fellow
fight
finally
find
first
flow
follow
fools
foot
for
forget
friend
friends
from
fruit

G

gentle
get
gifts
gives
giving
gloomy
goals
God
God's
gold
good
great
griping
guard

H

hands
happy
hard
harmful
harsh
have
he
healthful
heart
help
him
his
hold
honey
honor

I

insist
instead
if
in
is
it

J

judgment
just
justify

K

keep
keeps
kind
knowing
known

L

lazy
learn
lesson
let
lies
life
limp
long
looks
Lord
loving
loyal

M

make
man
many
me
medicine
mind
mirror
more
motives
much
must
my

N

name
need
never
nourished

O

obey
once
only
own

P

path
patient
peace
persuasive
please
pleased
pleasure
possession
precious
proud
pull
punishes
pure
put
putting

Q

quarrel
quarreling
quarrels

R

rather
really
reflects
reputation
results
returns
reverence
riches
right
run

S

safe
satisfaction
seems
self
sense
sensible
sharp
shooting
shown
sick
sidetrack
silver
slip
slow
soft
someone
son
soul
speech
spirit
starts
starve
stay
step
stick
stop
stumble
succeed
success
sure
sword

T

take
talk
telling
tempered
than
the
thing
those
tightly
time
tongue
too
tree
trouble
true
trust
truth
truthful
trying
turn
two

U

understanding

V

virtues

W

want
watch
ways
we
what
when
whether
who
will
wisdom
wise
wisest
within
wonderful
word
work
worst
would
wounding
wrath
write
wrong

Y

you
your
yourself

Skills List Index — "Words of Wisdom"

These alphabet letters emphasized for practice may be found on the following pages.

Ways to Share

Most students enjoy writing their verses on the special Scripture border sheets and then decorating them. But even more, they should find satisfaction in sharing these gems from Scripture.

Sending the verses home with the students can be a real blessing to their families. But for variety, why not sponsor an outreach activity in which the entire class can participate at least once a month?

Here are some suggestions for ways students can share their verses. A classroom should be able to discover several additional ways, too!

Ways to Share:

- Put the verse in a place where members of the family will see it every day. Suggest the door of the refrigerator or a common bulletin board.

- Send the Scripture border sheet to work with a parent to share with fellow employees.

- Give the page to grandparents. (Encourage each student to include a personal message. The student can be given an extra Scripture border sheet to use for writing this letter; these can be purchased separately.)

- Share the verse with someone who works at the school—the secretary, janitor, groundskeeper, or principal.

- Encourage another Christian. (The church secretary could provide names of families in the congregation who would especially appreciate a special Scripture verse of encouragement.)

- If your students want to share their border sheets with a prisoner, you may call Concerned Communications at 1-501-549-9000 for the name & address of a prison ministries group that will forward the verse along with a letter without revealing the sender's address. Replies from the prisoner to the sender will be directed through the same group.

- Go to a nursing home, visit one patient, and leave the verse to decorate the room.

- Share the verse with a neighbor.

- Make a placemat. Center the Scripture border sheet on a large piece of construction paper or a plain paper placemat. Laminate the sheet or cover it with clear contact paper.

- Give the verse to someone who is sick. Hospitals may like to give verses to patients on their breakfast trays.

- Think of someone who is housebound. Deliver the verse in person, if possible.

Additional suggestions for teachers:

- Create an attractive bulletin board using Scripture border sheets. Or select the best each week and display it in a special place.

- If the school has a general display case, ask for permission to post Scripture border sheets from the class.

- See whether a church would like to display the best Scripture border sheets or enclose one with each copy of the church newsletter when it's mailed.

- Get a copy of church members' addresses. Go down the list, sending each family a Scripture border sheet with a personal note. Students will be delighted with the positive response this will generate!

- Send the best samples from the classroom to the publisher of *A REASON FOR WRITING* for possible display at educational conventions. Be sure to label each sheet (on the back) with the name, age, grade, and school of the student who created it.

Teachers and students have found that people receiving verses are more responsive when a letter describing the sharing program is sent with the verse. Mailing the letter on your school letterhead adds a nice touch. (See page 72 for a sample letter.)

Brainstorm with the class to add more suggestions to this list. The authors would like to hear about other ways of sharing. Please share with us!

Carol Ann Retzer & Eva Hoshino
c/o Concerned Communications
P. O. Box 1000
Siloam Springs, Arkansas 72761

Handwriting Evaluation Form

2 points possible for each:

Alignment
Letter stays on the line.   _____

Slant
Letters have the same slant.   _____

Size
Capital and lowercase letters
are the right size.   _____

Shape
Letters are shaped correctly
and neatly.   _____

Spacing
Letters and words are spaced
and spelled correctly.   _____

TOTAL   _____

Handwriting Evaluation Form

2 points possible for each:

Alignment
Letter stays on the line.   _____

Slant
Letters have the same slant.   _____

Size
Capital and lowercase letters
are the right size.   _____

Shape
Letters are shaped correctly
and neatly.   _____

Spacing
Letters and words are spaced
and spelled correctly.   _____

TOTAL   _____

Handwriting Evaluation Form

2 points possible for each:

Alignment
Letter stays on the line.   _____

Slant
Letters have the same slant.   _____

Size
Capital and lowercase letters
are the right size.   _____

Shape
Letters are shaped correctly
and neatly.   _____

Spacing
Letters and words are spaced
and spelled correctly.   _____

TOTAL   _____

Handwriting Evaluation Form

2 points possible for each:

Alignment
Letter stays on the line.   _____

Slant
Letters have the same slant.   _____

Size
Capital and lowercase letters
are the right size.   _____

Shape
Letters are shaped correctly
and neatly.   _____

Spacing
Letters and words are spaced
and spelled correctly.   _____

TOTAL   _____

A Reason For Writing

Scripture Verses That Make Handwriting Fun!

Kindergarten

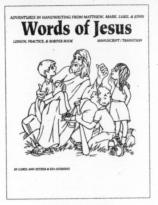
1st Grade

Words of Jesus
2nd Grade

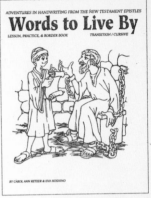
3rd Grade

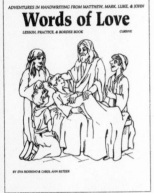
4th Grade

5th Grade

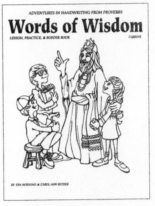
6th Grade

Teacher's Guide

Additional Classroom Teaching Aids:

Alphabet Wall Sheets

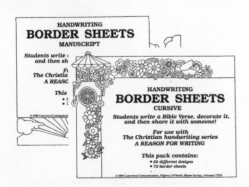
Extra Border Sheets

Student Alphabet Desk Cards